COACHING
IN
COMMUNITIES

COACHING

—— IN ——

COMMUNITIES

PURSUING JUSTICE,
TEACHER LEARNING,
AND TRANSFORMATION

Melissa Mosley Wetzel
Erica Holyoke
Kerry H. Alexander
Heather Dunham
Claire Collins

Harvard Education Press
Cambridge, MA

Paperback ISBN: 978-1-68253-819-7

Library of Congress Cataloging-in-Publication Data is on file.

Published by Harvard Education Press,
an imprint of the Harvard Education Publishing Group
Harvard Education Press
8 Story Street
Cambridge, MA 02138

Cover Design: Endpaper Studio
Cover Image: Watercolor courtesy of Kerry H. Alexander / www.languageartistry.com

The typefaces in this book are Adobe Garamond Pro, Helvetica Neue, and Trade Gothic

*To the beautiful children and young people
who have been our teachers,
and to the teachers who have nurtured one another,
and their learners, through coaching*

CONTENTS

CHAPTER 1

JUSTICE-FOCUSED COACHING

In preparing teachers for educating all learners, experts have frequently used one common support: coaching.[1] Historically, coaching has been described as something an expert does *for* teachers. The coaching is focused either on fidelity—helping teachers learn a new curriculum or instructional practice to do it effectively—or on helping teachers learn from practice so that they can see what works for learners, and why. In the United States, systems of education have often prioritized such conformity, accountability, and standards over the goal of creating environments that are more just and fair to help disrupt systemic and structural inequities. Teachers therefore might not have the coaching tools they need to pursue justice.

Misty Sailors and James V. Hoffman, in a literacy leadership brief written for the International Literacy Association in 2019, describe another way to think about coaching—coaching for transformation.[2] This approach focuses on what is possible in terms of societal change and what is hopeful. This is the coaching that teachers need today. In this book, we argue that to coach for transformation, teachers need to redefine coaching as something done in community to learn together and focus on addressing inequities in schools. Gloria Ladson-Billings, whose theories of culturally relevant pedagogy and critical race theory have influenced the field of teacher education and teaching, recently suggested that teachers and teacher educators turn their attention from

1

"social justice" to "just justice" matters with urgency in response to daily egregious injustices, through a practice of reflection and action.[3] The strong backlash from conservative legislators and the public to a focus on justice suggests that these justice-focused approaches are beginning to have an impact on upending White supremacy.[4] In this book, as teachers and coaches, we forge ahead and follow Ladson-Billings's lead in developing a framework for justice-focused coaching in solidarity. We argue that justice-focused coaching, based on research, can assist communities working toward equity.

In an eight-year study, one of us (Melissa) collaborated with colleagues at the University of Texas to design a model for coaching in preservice teacher education.[5] The model, called Coaching with CARE (for content, appreciative, reflexive, and experiential) is a responsive approach to coaching. With this approach, the coach considers the assets of culturally and linguistically diverse learners and clearly identifies and appreciates strategies for teaching. Reflective coaching disrupts the everyday ways of teaching; for example, by directly addressing critical social issues. Coaching with CARE draws from the traditions of coaching—behavioral, cognitive, humanistic, and critical—because not every coaching situation is the same and not every teacher being coached, and not every coach, draws on the same traditions. The CARE model is also relational: coaching occurs in the community of the local classroom and develops in a community of coaches who are building their practice. Relational coaching is based on the scholarship of Nel Noddings, Rosalie Rolón-Dow, and Angela Valenzuela, who theorized that care occurs at the level of caring *for* the person being mentored and caring *with* the person about issues of justice and equity in relation to learners.[6]

Coaching with CARE responds to the shortcomings of models of coaching in preservice teacher education. Namely, preservice teachers are often positioned as apprentices of practice who learn through transmission not to transform education but to fit in. Supposed experts are called in to coach without preparation and often end up coaching in ways that maintain the status quo. The consequences of this shortsighted approach include academic learning that is divorced from people's lives and histories, and teachers who work from deficit perspectives. Consequently, learners with mostly White, Eurocentric, English-language-centered ways of talking, learning, and behaving become the achievers. The status quo means that many learners and teachers fail to thrive because so many are excluded from opportunity. When we, as researchers, embarked on the project one decade ago, few had investigated how coaching can challenge the status quo. We conducted discourse analyses of coaching conversations, studied the ways coaches changed their practices when they reflected on their coaching, and learned how coaches interrupt racism, sexism, and dominant deficit ways of positioning learners in a reflective coaching conversation. One of our significant findings was that coaching can help teachers to create (and continually revise) practices for disruption and to have critical conversations to build more equitable classrooms and schools.

We find ourselves writing about coaching in a time of urgency for the teaching profession—during a teaching shortage that could be devastating to our communities, which depend on a strong teaching force. The Economic Policy Institute conducted a set of studies on teacher attrition, citing the shortage of teachers as a problem inadequately understood or addressed in education. The report concluded, "The teacher shortage makes it more difficult to build a solid reputation for teaching and to professionalize it, which further contributes to perpetuating the shortage."[7] This teacher shortage, then, impacts all stakeholders in the field.

Research also indicates that the teacher shortage does not affect all learners and communities equally. The shortage disproportionately hurts communities of Color.[8] And there continue to be long-lasting ramifications of the whitening pool of administrators and teachers, a trend often traced to, and stemming from, *Brown v. Board of Education.*[9] The inadequate supply of teachers threatens both the profession and learners because districts are often forced to fill vacancies with teachers who are not certified. Systems of education, especially those that serve communities of Black, Indigenous, and People of Color (BIPOC), refugees, and recent arrivals to the United States, have become more deficit-oriented and more standardized, creating pressure chambers that have no release valve. Learners of Color in schools in communities experiencing the most devastating effects of racial injustice, climate change, health challenges, and so on, have also been denied a curriculum that is centered on, and directed by, their cultural wealth and experiences.

In this new context, we explore what kinds of coaching are needed for transformation. Our author team is also new—a research group composed of Melissa, Erica, Kerry, Heather, and Claire. Together, we conducted research on coaching and teacher learning, bringing principles from Coaching with CARE into new settings, before and during a global pandemic. Our audience has expanded from preservice teachers to include school-based literacy coaches who work with in-service teachers and teachers who coach their peers in inquiry groups. This book also addresses how coaching might also alleviate the challenge of the teacher shortage. As we continue to wade through injustices in schools and society—injustices such as racism, linguicism, and a deprofessionalization of teaching, all of which politically separate schools from communities—we address the *what* of justice-focused coaching. We discuss how teachers work alongside learners and their families, within and outside classroom walls, to challenge inequities. We also connect the *why* of justice-focused coaching, or the need to disrupt the systems of oppression that hurt our learners and their communities. These oppressive systems include racial violence and the marginalization of people's lived experiences and values.

PERSPECTIVES THAT GUIDE US

We thought quite a bit about what we would call our framework for coaching, because we have committed to movements marked by the terms *social change, transformation,* and *social justice.* Words matter, and we seek both to extend and to build on the long histories of scholars and activists who have engaged in these movements. In solidarity with Ladson-Billings, we decided on the word *justice,* as it puts us into both historical and contemporary conversations about to the immediacy of addressing and dismantling oppression. We also follow Elena Aguilar, who has developed coaching for transformation, a justice-focused framework for coaching in schools, and Misty Sailors and Logan Manning, who propose justice-focused coaching in line with the coaching for transformation framework we described earlier in this chapter.[10] In this section, we provide an overview of the theoretical perspectives that guide us in the design of the justice-focused coaching tools we will share with you in this book. We start with how we define and theorize justice. We then turn to coaching and the perspectives on coaching we draw on and extend with a justice-focused approach. Of particular importance is our focus on critical self-reflection, or what Yolanda Sealey-Ruiz calls the archaeology of self, or the arch of self.[11] When coaching across boundaries of identity and context, each person is responsible for investigating their own racial and social positions, histories, and trajectories.

When we talk about justice, we are referring to the dismantling of systems that lead to unearned privileges and oppression. Activists have long centered the liberation of those who experience oppression, which is tied up with the liberation of those who live with and benefit from the unearned privileges in society. Justice is not an endpoint; it is a process. Notions of equity and justice are intertwined. Justice means that all learners are supported to be successful in school and that schools expand notions of success to include culturally and linguistically diverse ways of life and learning. We critically examine what are called *achievement gaps* in light of what Ladson-Billings explained as an "education debt"—scrutinizing the differences between how White students and students of Color fare on high-stakes state-level assessments—through lenses of race, gender, class, and linguistic discrimination.[12]

The history of justice-focused work in education is long, and the story can be told from many perspectives. The story we ascribe to in this book is how justice has been pursued over time and with persistence by communities despite, and working against, the tides of power. Schools often use measures such as test scores, attendance rates, graduation rates, and grades to measure their success in educating learners. However, across those in the profession, there is no clear agreement that these measures reflect the values of all stakeholders in education. Some stakeholders would like to know whether learners see their education as an added value to their lives and livelihoods or how much the knowledge and practices of their communities are reflected in the curriculum. Kristien Zenkov conducted a study asking learners from urban schools to create a photo documentation project showing what they wanted their teachers to know about them.[13] He found that they wanted to be cared for and mentored, and they wanted their teachers to sustain hope regarding their future success. These metrics are quite different from those currently used to evaluate teachers and teaching.[14] The profession will need metrics that look beyond individual learners to community health and well-being to contextualize equity and inequity in schools. We ascribe to a story that we hope will turn stakeholders' collective focus to issues of personhood, curriculum, and instruction instead of measuring learners.

Justice in education also is a matter of recognizing the ways that curriculum in schools has always privileged Whiteness and White ways of knowing. This privilege has been expanded by scholars through theories such as languagelessness, anti-Blackness, systemic tracking, linguistic assimilation, and subjugation, all of which were historically and are presently manifest in experiential, cultural, and social segregation.[15] Jennifer Adair and Kiyomi Sánchez-Suzuki Colegrove write: "We are all responsible for removing what Charles Mills calls the personhood–sub-personhood line that justifies some receiving freely what others have to earn or demonstrate worthiness in order to receive." Justice means engaging with these truths with fervor, but for many (if not most) White teachers, this way of speaking, acting, and doing feels highly unfamiliar and leaves the teacher feeling emotional and vulnerable.[16]

To do something different, we need to reflect on injustice and recognize when the curriculum privileges the stories and texts written by White authors and historians. For example, teachers must notice libraries of books mostly in English in communities where English is the second or third language of most families and name this linguistic bias. When teachers hear other teachers and administrators correcting language practices that reflect learners' lived experiences, they need the tools to interrupt and restore the personhood of the learner. When learners are sent out of classrooms, teachers need to draw on Maisha Winn's observation on how BIPOC children and youth are hurt by punitive discipline systems that privilege being right over making things right.[17] Teacher educators will need to follow Marcelle Haddix, Bree Picower, and Rita Kohli, who know that the teacher education programs and opportunities for teacher learning have neither properly prepared White teachers nor drawn on the expertise and critical knowledge of teachers of Color.[18]

In this book, we define a culturally responsive curriculum, again drawing on Ladson-Billings's work, as a curriculum that is rigorous and reflects the variety of cultural practices that make our schools and society diverse and beautiful. A culturally responsive curriculum honors learners' lived experiences and builds on the critical consciousness they bring to classrooms. It centers the perspectives and input of families and sees families as partners in education. Django Paris and H. Samy Alim's culturally sustaining pedagogy disrupts the persistent and continuous nature of a curriculum that upholds White normativity, racism and disparate outcomes for children and youth of Color with a call for more equitable practices.[19]

Critical literacies are another approach that counters deficit perspectives and the policing of learners' ways of talking, learning, and being. During the school day, learners have fewer and fewer opportunities to talk about their connections to, and disconnections from, texts and to practice the critical literacies that have been fundamental in movements for social change.[20] Critical literacies address learners across the lifespan—including the youngest learners—and recruit them in the creation of new designs for learning. The new designs are often seen in a project-based and inquiry curriculum, in which learners produce and act in ways that influence and change oppressive practices. Critical literacies align with critical race perspectives, centering the development of counter stories to point out issues of race and power.[21]

In this book, you'll hear our stories as we worked alongside educational advocates and activists in justice-focused programs and inquiry groups to initiate change through embodied activism. These groups are spaces of collective learning and action for teachers who share similar commitments. Justice means that not only do activists and teachers act to disrupt systems that continue to lead to inequalities, but those actions are embedded in institutions. For example, a school district that regularly conducts equity audits to understand how policies are affecting BIPOC in the system and then changes to remediate the inequities would be an example of pursuing justice.[22]

We hope it will be apparent that justice-focused projects in early childhood and K–12 classrooms require a continual, laborious process. Throughout a school year, as you meet with other teachers and coach one another through practice, you will have to scrutinize the curriculum and use critical perspectives to examine your own participation in systems of oppression. You will have to listen to community members who you might not be accustomed to hearing. To build relationships, you might collaborate on a project that is not squarely in your usual area of focus. You may come to see that what is a culturally responsive curriculum for you is not a match with what families want for their children, and you will have to contend with those conflicts. You might be interrupted when high-stakes testing preparation pushes in. And you might find that to do so creates a new struggle to prepare learners for access to codes of power.[23]

To engage with justice means struggling, and you will not be satisfied with this book if you hope to find answers. Rather, we hope you are ready for unlearning and disentangling your own participation in the oppressive system of schooling. Teachers who have endeavored to work in communities in these ways face struggles that are both personal and political. For example, Myles Horton at the Highlander Research and Education Center in New Market, Tennessee, was an adult educator.[24] He had a theory of how problems would be solved when people who shared expertise together conceptualized change. He understood that collaboration means we are not apprenticing one another into fixed roles but are instead always forging new ground together. He looked for practices that honored both the individual knowledge of people and the collective goals of systemic change. Using practices such as conversation circles, with all stakeholders facing one another, and shared inquiry, Horton and his partners disrupted Black voter suppression and unequal pay for Black laborers. These networks of support took time to build, and there was a long process of developing trust. Eventually, reciprocating learning networks were formed, and they created the accountability needed for each person to face the discomfort and unfamiliarity that social change can produce.

Finally, in our conception of justice, we need to address the notion of feedback. This buzzword in education usually means that someone with supposedly more expertise in educating learners provides direction to one who is more novice. Justice is not compatible with these hierarchies of power. If teachers want feedback, they need to turn their attention to learners, their families, and the communities they are accountable to. As a teacher and a person, you must accept, with humility, that you will not always get things right in the classroom—such is the nature of teaching. When learners and their families are our feedback, we have the privilege and opportunity to attend to their excitement, engagement, resistance, and care for materials and each other. The true work of justice is collaborative, sustained engagement in resistance to the oppressive systems we face.

COACHING FROM A VARIETY OF PERSPECTIVES

Early in this chapter, we proposed that in coaching, people may not have the tools they need to pursue justice. In fact, even when equity is at the center of the model, coaching is often pursued from cognitive and behavioral perspectives that focus on changing a teacher's beliefs and practices. From a behaviorist perspective, coaching can increase a teacher's assessment in their teaching and can set goals related to performance or actions. Coaching can assist a teacher in becoming more self-aware, more efficacious, and better at teaching. Typically, behavioral perspectives draw on modeling or rubrics that help the coach and teacher to home in on areas of growth or change, both professional and pedagogical. A cognitive or cognitive-behavioral perspective additionally focuses on the development of the teacher's ability to observe his or her own behavior, to identify the outcomes of those actions, to set meaningful goals for action, and to evaluate or think through the process of change. Again, coaching from this perspective would rely on a rubric or framework for particular teaching practices and professional competencies in the classroom.

An alternative method of coaching draws on these cognitive and behavioral perspectives but centers on the personhood of those being coached. Referred to as *humanistic coaching* in the field of psychology, this approach focuses more on the individual goals and perspectives of the teacher being coached. Jane Gregory and Paul Levy, in a review of this perspective, write that the tenets of humanistic coaching include six elements: (1) an assumption that the client can be their full or authentic self; (2) a focus on positivity and the client's well-being; (3) an emphasis on the client's growth, development, and maximizing potential; (4) a focus on goal-directed and intentional behavior; (5) the nondirective role of the coach; and (6) the importance of the coaching relationship.[25]

A humanistic perspective centers on the thoughts, feelings, and emotions of the person being coached. The coach is nondirective, meaning they put coaching goals aside, as well as rubrics or expectations, to understand the teaching and learning process from the perspective of the person being coached. Sometimes coaches can employ humanistic approaches within a more traditional model, but they might feel tensions between a person-centered approach and one that includes more directive or evaluative components.

For a coach working from the humanistic perspective, the relationship of the coach to the teacher comes first. One of us (Erica) described her perspective on coaching in both the preservice context and as a novice teacher mentor:

> Some of the ways to build relationships include informal check-ins, consistency (this has always been something I have found to build trust quickly), and, importantly, following the lead of the person being observed. That means putting aside coaching agendas and encouraging space for the teacher to share openly and co-construct. I've also found it to be valuable to be vulnerable as a coach and to repeat back what matters to the mentee, while also highlighting their strengths. I find that shining a light on their strengths, while also amplifying their

think-alouds, focuses, wonderings offers a strong foundation for a relationship both in person and in virtual contexts.

We have often privileged the humanistic perspective in Coaching with CARE.[26]

Another perspective on coaching, different from behavioral, cognitive, and humanistic, is a critical perspective. This perspective, as discussed by Noddings, Rolón-Dow, and Valenzuela, is often located in peer relationships because the focus of the coaching shifts from caring *for* the person being coached to caring *with* the person. Under this perspective, the person being coached is actively engaged with others in making changes in the classroom and beyond those walls. Critical coaching is squarely focused on equity and justice for learners and their communities, with one another, and with those whom the teachers serve.

Critical coaching builds on each of these perspectives but stresses a critical view of educational systems, social structures, and inequities related to race, gender, sexuality, nationality, status of citizenship, language, ability, and access. Drawing from Elena Aguilar, the critical coaching perspective requires you not only to understand a model but also to have done the work to understand your own histories and perspectives and how your identity, such as race or gender, has provided or restricted critical ways of knowing.[27] Whereas humanistic coaching is focused on the teacher as human, critical coaching is concerned with humanizing pedagogies that extend to all those who are affected by teaching decisions.

Critical coaching requires attention in times when there is great social upheaval or in moments like this one, as technology and communications advance, health and environmental concerns swell, and racial and political tensions and violence have shaken us, as teachers and parents, and community members, to the core. Teachers are at the center of these complex problems, as they witness the impact of our society's thorny problems like racism, sexism, and intolerance on learners' bodies, hearts, and minds. Coaching can speak directly to these structural inequities and attitudes of White supremacy and individualism that hold them in place. Teachers cannot wish these problems away and "just teach." To be an educator means working with and through the problems as they arise, open to the possibility that we are complicit in upholding such inequities. Critical coaching means each person works alongside those who have experienced the oppressions they hope to disrupt and those who experience oppressions differently.

JUSTICE-FOCUSED COACHING: A NEW PERSPECTIVE

Justice-focused coaching has more than simply a critical perspective: other perspectives are not ignored or excluded. Rather, like teaching, coaching with a justice focus requires coaches to have access to many tools and know how to apply them with thoughtfulness and reflection. Justice-focused coaching is twofold, and we expand on these two meanings throughout this book: disrupting expert-novice divides and coaching in community.

First, we redefine coaching to *disrupt expert–novice divides.* Experts often have positions of power, meaning they are in a role to evaluate others and have earned those positions because of their effectiveness in practice. Instructional coaches are highly effective teachers, for example, and field supervisors are experienced teachers. However, justice-focused coaching is often aimed at transforming educational systems that are unjust. It is often difficult for those who have been successful and high-achieving in such systems to locate those inequities. Justice-focused coaching centrally uses language and other practices to build community, disrupting terms such as *coach* or *novice* by positioning everyone, always, as learners and co-inquirers. By disrupting expert–novice divides, we open new possibilities that are more imaginative and transformative. A justice-focused coach must shift from an apprenticeship approach, which reifies existing structures, to one of collaboration.

Studies of coaching have often relied on a model promoting a gradual release of responsibility. The model focuses on the gradual withdrawal of support as the learner takes on more effort, independent of the teacher or coach.[28] Such a model privileges expertise and reifies power relations. It is not "I do, we do, you do." It is always "we do." Vicki Collet retools this model of coaching.[29] In a study of coaching, she describes an "increase of responsibility model" as an alternative to gradual release: "The model shows teachers' gradually increasing interdependence and collaboration as they rely less on the coach and engage more in collaboration."

Second, justice-focused coaching within community also leads teachers to partner with communities and draw on the knowledge and expertise of learners and their families therein, to engage in horizontal expertise. With this type of coaching, teachers must be conscious of subjectivities and identities that are related to their values.[30] White teachers, who may lack access to the wealth of knowledge held by communities of Color regarding what justice looks like and sounds like, must also unlearn much of what they have been taught. This unlearning of their own beliefs, combined with their honoring of the knowledge that others bring, is a cornerstone of justice-focused work. In the other perspectives we have discussed, there are clear roles for the coach and the person being coached. These other approaches repeat the expert–novice binary, a distinction that is concerning. The disruption of these binaries is what mainly distinguishes justice-based coaching from earlier approaches.

Also, justice-focused coaching is *contextual and based in communities working for change.* Critical race scholars such as Ladson-Billings and advocates of justice-focused teacher education such as Detra Price-Dennis, Sealey-Ruiz, Haddix, Picower, and Kohli highlight the stories and experiences of teachers of Color to point out that issues of race and power are always relevant in education. Coaching relies on having a strong justice framework so that teachers can identify their own limitations, understand where critical social issues are in the curriculum and history of the school, and transform education through coaching.

We also propose that coaching for justice must take advantage of the momentum of existing efforts toward change. Jeffrey Duncan-Andrade's observations of inquiry groups that focused bringing about justice in their classrooms and communities inform our thinking about how teachers reach beyond the silos they often experience in their classrooms, finding others who are similarly invested in change.[31] Scholarship addressing this question often focuses on the collaboration of teachers in a professional community in which knowledge is built, adapted, and shared. Change does not happen in one classroom, for one teacher, but comes when teachers collaborate to agitate systems for transformation. Paulo Freire argues that when teachers want to dismantle oppression, they must start with the education of those who have been oppressed.[32] We will charge you, the readers, to empower one another through your relationships and collective learning toward change.

Justice-focused coaching must encompass both meanings of justice-focused coaching by directly challenging notions of power and expertise, supporting culturally relevant and sustaining practices, and building on movements to decenter Whiteness in education. Coaching for justice is not new. However, to date, we have not found a resource that supports coaching for justice across preservice and in-service environments and considers justice-focused coaching as a means to build communities. Furthermore, no literature has thus far evaluated how, and when, justice-focused coaching has been transformative for children, youth, their families, and the whole communities that are invested in them.

WHO WE ARE, AND WHO ARE WE WRITING FOR

The five of us are a research group bringing Coaching with CARE into new settings to learn about tools for justice, and we have long supported one another in building our own tool kits for justice-focused coaching. We have done research in the following settings, and we draw from these studies in each chapter of the book:

- In a preservice teacher education program at a large research-focused university, we prepare preservice teachers and their coaches, who include field supervisors and mentor teachers.
- In a master's degree program at the same university, we teach in-service teachers who are building capacities as literacy coaches and instructional leaders in their schools.
- In workshops supporting early-career teachers focused on coaching through a university-based induction program.
- In a summer program serving middle school youth, we support teachers and their coaches teaching in remote teaching settings.
- On the ground with local school community groups that include parents, caregivers, faculty, staff, and community leaders.
- In K–12 classrooms, we collaborate with teachers in shared inquiry and production and action with learners in their school and local communities.
- At local and national conferences, with teachers as our collaborators, we extend our research to larger audiences.
- Together with participants in our various projects, we create podcasts and other public resources that apply to coaching and mentoring in preservice and in-service situations.

We are fortunate to have the opportunities to join forces with a diversity of teachers across so many settings, and in our research, we have often found more similarities than differences in how various communities utilize justice-focused coaching. As an author team, we all identify as White women, much like the continued majority of the teaching force in public schools. We recognize that our identities have provided us privilege in many areas, including as teachers and leaders in educational settings. Throughout this book, we write scenarios derived from our research and coaching. It is important for us as authors, and you as readers, to examine the role of racial and other intersectional identities at play in the scenarios and how your own identities and experiences may vary. Here is who we are:

- *Melissa Mosley Wetzel, a professor and the department chair at the University of Texas at Austin:* I identify as a White woman and have mostly taught and prepared teachers in racially and linguistically diverse settings in the Midwest and in the southwestern United States. I have been preparing teachers in university settings for fifteen years. As a member of the literacy faculty, I teach courses to undergraduates who are learning to be teachers in field-based settings where coaching is used by course instructors, field supervisors, and cooperating teachers. My research has focused on coaching in these contexts. I have worked with in-service teachers and field supervisors to build their capacities for justice-focused coaching.
- *Erica Holyoke, an assistant professor in responsive literacy education at the University of Colorado Denver:* I identify as a White cis-gendered woman and strive to work as a racial accomplice in education and in my daily life. My research focuses on literacy, love, and justice in early childhood, elementary, and teacher preparation settings. I focus on the agency, creativity, and brilliance of teachers and children and how they put

these capacities to use through learning and justice-oriented pedagogies. I teach courses on building classroom communities, inclusive teaching, and literacy methods of instruction. As a former teacher, special educator, administrator, and literacy coach and currently as a teacher educator, I have learned from and alongside many young children and teachers about enacting equity-oriented teaching and coaching in schools.

- *Kerry H. Alexander, a current doctoral candidate in language and literacy studies at the University of Texas at Austin:* I identify as a White cis-gender woman. I study the pedagogical implications of, and alternatives to, White discourse patterning in literacy instruction and the impact of equity-focused community collaboration. For the past ten years, I have worked closely with one community as a parent, classroom literacy teacher, and researcher on how race, racism, and language are intertwined in ethics of care and success.

- *Heather Dunham, an assistant professor of literacy at Clemson University:* I identify as a White, monolingual woman who has taught elementary multilingual learners for five years. For the past three years, I have worked closely with preservice teachers in our elementary degree program as a field supervisor and instructor. My current research focuses on how teacher educators embed culturally sustaining practices into their coursework and how preservice teachers are able to take up these practices within their field experiences.

- *Claire Collins, a current doctoral candidate in language and literacy studies at the University of Texas at Austin:* As a White, cis-gender woman, I taught language arts to middle and high school learners in urban Catholic schools. Currently, I am examining my own work as a coach, learning alongside preservice teachers. My research looks at how coaches can form humanizing partnerships with preservice teachers built on dialogue and trust, while also negotiating the default hierarchy of the relationship that posits the coach as expert and the preservice teacher as novice. I am also interested in how secondary language arts teachers make decisions about literacy curricula that question the unequal social relations and power structures embedded in schools.

You the reader are an educator. You might be a candidate for licensure in a teacher education program or an experienced teacher; you might be a teacher educator. You might be a person who wants to either form or strengthen a network of support you have as an educator. We are writing to you, in whatever role you serve. Here are some audiences we imagine using this book:

- preservice teachers and their mentors in teacher education programs to develop coaching tools for field supervisors, course instructors, and cooperating teachers to use with preservice teachers
- in-service teachers and their mentors in more formal relationships such as instructional coaching roles
- in-service teachers in social-justice-focused inquiry groups that collaborate to improve practices
- in-service teachers who are looking for opportunities to grow their practice but do not have an assigned mentor or an inquiry group

These are just four examples of educators who would find this book important to use coaching as a tool for teacher learning.

Each of these groups has a different institutional context, and there are different requirements for those who serve as mentors and coaches. We will look at these contexts in our case studies and describe how formal evaluation systems can create tensions for justice-focused teachers. We will also show how coaching tools can be used in virtual environments that allow for collaboration when we are not physically together. Along these lines, you will also learn how coaching tools can provide more access to quality coaching for teachers in rural settings. Because these teachers face difficulties in commuting to places where they can collaborate, they need the support of adaptive technologies to participate in professional learning.

HOW THIS BOOK IS ORGANIZED

We hope you read this book with others, whether they are in your inquiry group, your grade-level team, or another setting. Along the way, we address recruiting a community to read together. You might take up each chapter of the book one at a time, with time between chapters try out some of the ideas in that chapter. This book should be a practical guide. We will refer to research and published literature to support you when you are asked to show that your approaches are based on evidence from research. After reading this book, you will want to be creative and build on this foundation in response to your local circumstances. We will be sure to orient you to the practical as well—what the tool is, how is it used, and how you can get started.

In this chapter, we have established justice-focused coaching as having two prongs: the disruption of expert–novice divides and the coach's direct connection with communities taking on justice together. We discussed the importance of theories on how classroom learners are regularly impeded by racism and structural and systemic inequities. Coaching relies on a strong justice framework so that teachers can identify their own limitations, understand critical social issues in the curriculum of the school, and transform education through coaching.

Chapter 2 will orient you to many of the perspectives we draw on throughout the book. We imagine you, the reader, also collaborating in multiracial, diverse communities that are working together for justice.

Chapters 3 and 4 focus on tools that communities use to coach one another. Chapter 5 builds on these tools and offers guidance on engaging in iterative, justice-focused cycles over time. When we began Coaching with CARE, we focused on the coaching cycles that are the heart of many teacher education programs, instructional coaching programs, and other ways that teacher learning is organized under the umbrella of coaching approaches. However, our research has eventually taught us that coaches who are justice-focused have a variety of daily tools in their tool kit. And we have learned that in many situations, a coaching cycle, which extends across multiple days, is not always feasible. Each tool is justice-focused on two levels: it disrupts the expert–novice distinctions that often obstruct learning in professional communities, and it leads the community to ask critical questions about inequities, access, and power in the classrooms they seek to transform. We address these two aspects in each chapter in the book. Throughout the chapters, we introduce and propose the many ways that coaching can leverage virtual tools to increase access and collaboration. Also responding to the current moment, this book addresses the immediate need for coaching that allows teachers to understand and resist current restrictive curriculum policies that will thwart their efforts to challenge inequities if not resisted.

Chapters 6 and 7 describe tools that extend beyond the daily coaching tools and that can ultimately be used to build justice-focused communities. We introduce how communities can use the coaching tools of empathy conversations and shared inquiry to build learning communities that are more just. In these two chapters, we emphasize building collective action through coaching to counter the well-worn pathways of coaching for proficiency and fidelity in classrooms. Both chapters are written for coaches and the larger communities working together to make change.

In chapter 8, we speak directly to you about how justice-focused coaching in communities is connected to larger systemic change. We talk more about the barriers and challenges that teachers face when initiating change, and how we see coaching as empowerment for teachers. We argue for professional commitments to communities and connect back to the theories that guide the practical aspects of the book. Drawing on our own professional experiences in collaborating with districts and communities, we encourage you to begin implementing justice-focused coaching into preservice and in-service programs rather than waiting to have full buy-in or support. The time is now, and we hope you are feeling energized to get started.

AN INVITATION

We are experts in the sense that we have done the research and have stories to tell from our ongoing collaborations with teachers and the communities they serve. However, we hope to disrupt an expert–novice divide as well in this book. We are always working on understanding our own shortcomings and the ways we benefit from, and reproduce, inequalities and privilege. You will hear our reflections throughout the pages of this book. We will also invite you to try, to reflect, and to revise your own coaching practices. Similarly, we will ask you to consider hard questions about position, power, and privilege. Reader, we know that, like the coaches we have worked with over time and who have been our teachers, you will move us all forward.

---- CHAPTER 2 ----

SPHERES OF INFLUENCE AND RIPPLES OF CHANGE

Justice-focused coaching, as we introduce in chapter 1, is a framework for learning in community to impact educational justice. The community you are considering when reading this book might be large or small; it might include teachers, leaders, mentors, families, and administrators. Most books about coaching do not provide this community-access point; rather, they are written for mentor teachers, instructional coaches, or teacher educators in coaching roles. Coaching in community requires a shared language and a shared philosophy or stance about the change a group of people wishes to make in a system.

In this chapter, we introduce two metaphors, spheres of influence and ripples of change. We believe these two ideas can focus a group of people who intend to work together for justice. We first heard these phrases used in our local district while attending Cultural Proficiency & Inclusivity workshops that Angela Ward had designed for teachers.[1]

Spheres of influence is a metaphor that refers to a person's most proximal social, institutional, and cultural systems of participation. In her sessions, Ward argues that antiracist work must depend on ripples of change across spheres of influence because schools and school systems operate in White-dominant, White-normative ways, which are kept in place by *people* who subscribe to those norms. Justice, therefore, depends on *each person* who participates in these systems to intentionally create ripples of change in networks over time. In this way, the term *ripples of change* refers to both the importance of the agentic self and the impetus, or force, of the collective. Ripples of change and spheres of influence have roots in organizational change theory and involve our social and professional networks, to varying degrees, in plans for strategic and intentional coaching in schools. In this chapter, we will also introduce you to several theories, including critical and racial literacies and language use, to illustrate how we extend the metaphor of ripples of change as practical acts of design and production.

To introduce the first metaphor, spheres of influence, we will share a conversation that two of us (Melissa and Kerry) had recently with a group of mentors and coaches to early-career teachers in the urban district we partner with at our university. This group of experienced teachers was hired by a collaborative team from the district and university, and many had recently left the classroom, although some had worked for years as consultants for literacy and equity initiatives. The director of the project holds office hours every Friday morning for one hour. They are held over Zoom, and Kerry and Melissa often attend as consultants on coaching. The group, diverse racially, ethnically, and in terms of years of experience, often starts by sharing how-it's-going stories about working with early-career teachers in the urban district. During the Covid-19 pandemic, the challenges of early-career teachers rose sharply and the stories were often about sadness, grief, frustration with the administration and policies of the state and district, and difficulties with communication.

On this day, one educator relayed a conversation she had recently with a mentee. The novice teacher was experiencing a great deal of stress about Covid-19 at the beginning of the school year: the district was staffed for three thousand more learners than were enrolled, an imbalance that leads to the reorganization of classes. The mentor relayed that when she asked the early-career teacher what she needed right now, she had answered, "A new governor," indicating frustration with the governor's policies that were affecting families' decisions: families sought to protect their children by keeping them physically out of schools, where restrictions and protections were misaligned with the level of spread in the community. Further, the policies were advocated by groups of mostly White, wealthy families who voiced opposition to mask mandates for children.

The mentor, a Latina educator who prioritizes equity and inclusion in her work with teachers and schools, told the early-career teacher, "Yes, but what is in our locus of control right now?" The mentor recognized that the policies in place were strongly unfair to Latinx communities in the schools served by this initiative. Her response was not sugarcoating the political difficulties facing the school community. She was referring to the layers of the spheres of influence that she and the mentee could focus on to initiate change and identifying points of action, reflection, and change close to the day-to-day work of teaching in the school.

The idea of ripples of change is the second metaphor we draw on in this chapter. In the previous example, the mentor asked the mentee to focus on a local area of control that they could change, while both women acknowledged the many layers of policy and practice that had affected the life of the classroom. *Ripples of change* refers to the ways teachers can focus on the local, the "locus of control," but still initiate change that eventually becomes more global through the accumulation of many small efforts. It refers to the radical acceptance of the stresses that affect our communities and the importance of keeping these needs (and our accountability) on the table.

At another Zoom meeting of this group in the late fall, Kerry and Melissa learned that the classrooms had been adjusted for the actual enrollment in the schools, and classrooms were fairly right-sized, with even numbers of learners. However, a lack of substitutes available in the district caused new constraints for teachers. When teachers took time off, the other teachers were covering one another's classes by either moving learners to new classrooms or moving teachers to new groups. Several of the mentors heard from the early-career teachers that the working conditions were becoming unjust, as they were often asked to supervise too many learners or were discouraged from using the personal time they were allotted in their contracts.

In response, some of the mentors focused at the most local level, relieving the early-career teachers' burden by coming into the classroom to teach while the mentees worked one-on-one with learners or connected with families. Other mentors, such as the educator we just quoted, advocated for the mentees' requests by speaking with campus administrators about the inequity of creating the strain of redistributing classes on early-career teachers. Each mentor took a different approach to how to consider spheres of influence. But together, they created a set of possible actions of support that would help the teachers adapt to (or resist) these constraints while advocating for the learners, their families, and the teachers. A district administrator who was present at the meeting listened to all these ideas, and the district initiated new partnerships to find support from family members, student teachers, and community members who were qualified to substitute-teach at the schools, further adding a ripple of change to support the integrity of the learning environments.

In these two examples, we illustrate how spheres of influence and ripples of change can shape our thinking about coaching in community—pursuing change with fellow teachers, administrators, parents, learners, teacher educators, and mentors. The examples also connect to the notions of radical acceptance of challenging situations and identifying collaborative change together. The remaining chapters contain practical coaching tools communities can use together. But first, we will explore how change is made in systems. These coaching tools are focused on the goal that all learners experience an education

that values their humanity and their diverse ways of knowing and being in the world and sets them up to thrive and be powerful change
agents in the world. Justice-focused coaching accomplishes this goal
by disrupting the power differentials between coaches and teachers,
initiating family and community collaboration, and placing equity
and justice at the center of each coaching event or experience. In this
chapter, we use these metaphors as a starting point for defining our
communities, where our action is aimed, and what that action might
look like for you in your own communities.

MOVING ACROSS LAYERS OF INFLUENCE

Joyce Epstein's use of spheres of influence emphasizes the intersections or overlaps between how the influences of family, community,
and school together shape learners' experiences.[2] The work of Project Zero at the Harvard Graduate School of Education extends the
metaphor to teachers working for change in their communities.[3] The
metaphor has a few key dimensions you can borrow as you consider
your own spheres of influence (we borrow everything in education!).
First, there are concentric circles starting with self and moving outward to include more individuals and contexts. The most local sphere
of influence is the self. Every person, as part of a community, can be
focused on growing and expanding themselves. At the most global
level, we might list additional aspects of a society that may seem very
distant from the local situation but that affect our professional lives.

The second feature is the movement from local to global and then
back to the local. The local-to-global movement represents what you
might see if you start with yourself and initiate ripples that move
outward and create broader and broader effects. You have likely felt
a responsibility to work across layers of these spheres of influence. As
teachers, we ask questions and build new theories in our classrooms
with our learners and with their families and then share that learning

with other educators through planning, creating a curriculum, and instruction. Each of us is a responsible learner and actor in a field that has traditionally privileged knowers, and in recognition of this privilege, we seek tools to alter these embedded ideologies as we go. However, researchers, policy makers, and even the media do influence what happens at more local levels, so there is an arrow moving from global to local as well.

In coaching for justice, teachers resist the tendency to privilege one layer of the spheres of influence over another. Rather, we as a group can identify the spheres of influence that have an impact on our teaching, our learners, and their communities. Also, we can use language and action in our local spaces to touch broader audiences. Let's think about how to create a diagram like the one in figure 2.1 for your own community.

Starting with the self, who are you? What identities do you bring to the community, and how are those identities foregrounded in light of the communities you're a part of? You might need to do the hard work of considering whether you hold a shared vision of equity with the other "selves"—learners and their families—who work for educational justice together. What elements of your identity are relevant in relation to others in your spheres? For instance, how might your conceptions of equity have been shaped by your physical, linguistic, and social experiences in schooling? How might these conceptions have shaped your decision-making as an educator?

Extending from self, you might next consider these questions: When you get together with other folks in your school or institution, who is present? Does your next sphere of influence include your closest educational colleague or colleagues? Or are there community members and learners who almost daily listen to your voice and share the same thoughts? Is there a teaching partner, a student teacher, a writing partner, or learners who you consider a part of this close layer

FIGURE 2.1 *The many layers in our spheres of influence*

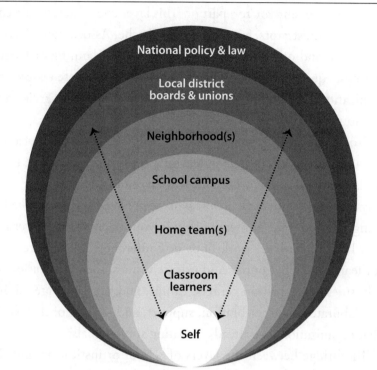

of the spheres of influence? Think of the people in this layer as your day-to-day thought partners.

The next layer is what you might call your home team, or your closest accountability partners. This group might be the teachers you most often work with to initiate change in your classroom—your confidants and critical friends. The home team is the group of people who most often hear you when you speak up about something that is on your mind and who may be the most willing to be called in to work with you for change. The group may be defined or undefined institutionally; it could be a grade-level team or a mentor.

You might next be looking more broadly at the school or institutional environment you're a part of. This layer could include the colleagues, administrators, families, Parent Teacher Associations (PTAs), counselors, and other support staff who attend planning or faculty meetings, equity councils, and community events. These people and organizations are bound together by a shared sense of service and community belonging.

From here, you might continue to think about which local organizations support teachers in teaching for justice. The more times you ask yourself about who is in this layer of influence, the more likely you'll be to identify people who may have been overlooked as having a shared stake or membership in your community. For example, what district-level workshops or conferences are resources for your learning? What public and private venues, such as libraries, local businesses, recreation centers, camps, and museums are willing to collaborate in the celebration, support, and sharing of this work? What organizations are already pursuing similar goals?

The bridge between the layers of school or institution and the more global layers might be identified as the geographical community. How do you define the community of the school? Our colleague Haydee Rodriguez at the University of Texas at Austin has a long history of locating community spheres of influence with preservice and in-service teachers at a school near the university.[4] The school is in a historically Latinx community that has been gentrified over time. She takes teachers on neighborhood walks to meet and visit with community members who can offer historical perspectives and a critical analysis of how the neighborhood has changed. The restaurant owner, the baker, and the religious leaders share their perspectives with teachers as well as their hopes and dreams for the children and youth who are the heart of this neighborhood. They speak about the meanings of art and murals in the neighborhood and how they represent these hopes and dreams. You can come to know your community spheres of influences through these types of activities and practices.

At the more global levels, you may have to make more choices about how you consider your spheres of influence. For our early-career mentors, the spheres relevant to coaching included the school boards that set policies in the district—policies that were influenced by the local school community but more importantly by the diverse interests of families in a large urban district. These spheres of influence also included media—for instance, in the ways that television and radio pundits and journalists use language and image to influence the public. The mentors may also have been influenced by social media and how their online networks engaged in critical professional discourse together. The question here is, Who is your wider community and education community that shape your understanding of justice?

PAUSE AND REFLECT

Consider mapping spheres of influence with your closest colleagues and mentees. Grab some breakfast tacos (we are from Texas), your writer's notebooks, and some colored pencils to make a map of who you know and the systems that influence local policy. Use table 2.1 as a question guide. You will coach one another through sticky situations in this project, asking each other, "Who else?" This map will continue to be useful for your group as you learn about coaching tools such as empathy conversations and shared inquiry.

Throughout this book, we refer to coaching as one of the ways change is initiated across spheres of influence. Learning continues because all teachers and community members hold expertise. At different moments, coaches can ask good questions, provide others with opportunities with support and challenge, and engage each other in new perspectives. In this case, teachers, coaches, and community members do the work to cultivate social solidarity in our schools and

TABLE 2.1 *Groundwork for spheres of influence: Journaling questions*

SELF	Begin with yourself. Who are you? What social identities do you hold and express? What roles do you take on in your community space?
CLASSROOM	Who are your learners? What social identities do they hold and express? Who are the people in *their* spheres of influence? How have you brought learners and families into the work of educational justice in this space? How might you do so?
HOME TEAM(S)	Who might you consider your justice-focused accountability partners? How have you supported one another in this critical endeavor? How might you support one another better? Consider co-teachers, team members, university colleagues, field supervisors, and preservice teachers.
SCHOOL CAMPUS	Who are the colleagues, administrators, family members, counselors, and support staff who attend planning or faculty meetings, equity councils, and community events? How is institutional power distributed in these relationships? How do stakeholders share their thoughts and concerns at this level?
NEIGHBORHOOD(S)	What local organizations support educators in teaching for justice? Who are the folks involved in this work? Include stakeholders from public and private venues, such as libraries, coffee shops, recreation centers, afterschool programs, and museums. Who might be willing to collaborate in learning, support, and sharing in this work?
LOCAL DISTRICT AND MEDIA SPACES	Compile a list of district specialists, union advocates, trustees, and board members. Language use and imagery are particularly salient in this sphere. What and how do text threads, critical professional learning, and Twitter chats reflect community interests? Who are the voices, and which images hold the most power here? Whose voices seem to be missing from the conversations? What stories are currently circulating?
NATIONAL POLICY AND LAW ARTIFACTS	What artifacts—laws, bills, and initiatives—influence your community and local schools? What are current research trends? Who writes, shapes, and evaluates the laws that dictate instruction in our classrooms? Consider lawmakers, education agencies, and university research teams. What alliances and partnerships are available for collaborative learning?

institutions. To engage these tools is to willingly embody justice work as a critical component of responsible education.

Further, although we start with self-reflection in the spheres-of-influence exercise, the tool is a lens to help us make meaning of our surroundings and take intentional action toward justice in schools. In US public schools, teaching and learning have often been oriented toward individualism and have been deeply entangled with perspectives of Whiteness. By changing our orientation when examining the spheres of influence, we blur the lines between the various spheres. This blurring helps us think deeply about the interconnections within and across communities and leads us to strive for justice *and* deemphasize individualism and White perspectives in education.

CHANGE BEGETS CHANGE

How do you change things in more local spaces, and how does this change affect things at more global levels? To talk about ripples of change, we need to talk about production and action. Initially, we thought of production and action as a coaching tool. However, as we explored production and action in our writing, we realized that productions can *activate* change. We produce new things every day, and when we are teaching, these productions vary in impact from very local to more global.

Let's dig into this continuum from local to global a bit more. Local is related to the location you hold as a person in an institution. If you are a teacher, your local position when you are teaching is a classroom. Your local community is the people you see, touch, and hear day-to-day. Your local influence is most salient here in the classroom, but your influence also ripples out to the folks who are touched by your work there. These people include the learners' siblings, families, and caregivers; other teachers who see, touch, and hear the learners in your classroom each day; religious leaders; and youth leaders. When you shift your practice in the classroom, you make changes that are somewhat predictable and knowable. Because of this predictability, you may have more control over the dissemination and impact of your decisions.

Many theorists suggest that we often focus on the local meanings of our actions in the world because those are the effects we can follow most easily.[5] However, our actions are also global in two ways. First, we know that each of us holds a set of theories that direct our work in the world. As James Gee writes, we often think of theory as something produced by experts, writers, and philosophers.[6] However, "people hold theories about all sorts of things, because in many cases . . . people's beliefs (and even prejudices) hang together and cohere in ways that are certainly like theories." Because theories often seem like something more formal or concrete, we go with Gee's term *storylines*, which connect what we do in local spaces with more global ways of knowing and acting in the world.

Teachers often live within and through storylines that are so well worn and commonplace that it is hard to recognize or know how to thoughtfully revise them. During the pandemic, when instruction transitioned to conferencing apps and webinars on remote learning, many common storylines were exposed as insufficient or inequitable. Some of the ones we relied on most, such as our deeply held beliefs about student and family-centered learning and equity, took priority. At the same time, we began to see teaching become less contextually relevant and more connected to school-district-mandated curricula, standardized instruction, and so on. In ways that may have been less visible to teachers before these shifts, the pandemic amplified the tremendous inequalities that existed and the impossibility of addressing these inequalities through quick fixes.

How do educational theorists consider local changes that influence the global sphere, especially when these changes seem too big or overwhelming? Here, we draw on critical and racial literacies to present two theories that can help explain ripples of change as local actions to both understand and disrupt storylines that guide teachers. As discussed earlier, people show critical literacy when they seek to identify dominant perspectives and their influence and to change oppressive practices. Critical literacies are ways of reading content—whether it is written, visual, multimodal, or multimedia—with a critical lens, asking how the material either promotes or disrupts oppression. Theorist Hilary Janks describes critical literacies as ways of exploring the many inequities in schools, such as standardizing language policies.[7] People with critical literacies understand the dominant ways of communicating in any place or situation and what is necessary to participate in those practices. She emphasizes that having access to these literacies of power is not the goal of critical literacies, but rather, it is to disrupt and expand those literacies so they are more available to all. Researchers have studied critical literacies across global contexts and with very young children, youth, and adults.[8] For example, a teacher can show critical literacy by reading all material, including images, with questions about justice in mind and by bringing unrepresented visitors—such as school staff, community elders, and historians—into the classroom.

Janks also puts forth the use of critical literacies to design or tell more complex or liberatory stories of how race and power work in the world. *Design* can mean making murals, protest signs, posters, and other media to promote justice or partnering with local businesses to create and provide resources about justice. Design is the earnest recognition of both the inequitable practices in our local spheres and the new possibilities that will be more equitable and just. Janks writes about the importance of design in developing critical consciousness; that is, the ability to see the complexities of social inequalities in relation to identities and experiences of different people. From a critical literacies perspective, design means using language and other ways of communicating to produce and act in the world. In doing so, we change ourselves and others in ways that may seem small, but Janks emphasizes that we need design to avoid being stuck in the land of critique without imagining something else.

Critical literacies are related to racial literacies and help us explain how a person becomes (and is always becoming) anti-racist. From Sealey-Ruiz's perspective, racial literacies begin with excavating one's own histories and participation as racialized people, extending critical literacies to center a framework of race.[9] Racial literacies, like critical literacies, emphasize design for critical consciousness. In their book on racial and digital literacies, Price-Dennis and Sealey-Ruiz argue that through our productions, we demonstrate racial literacies, using the diverse language and cultural resources we bring from a pluralistic, racially diverse society into our productions.[10] Racial literacies demand a recognition of the ways Eurocentrism (the basis of traditional schooling) is prioritized in many educational spaces, but it is only one way of knowing and clearly has been the most powerful and harmful when it encounters diversity and differences. Racial literacies bring attention to the ways that race and racism are embedded in the fabric of our institutions and society. In classrooms, children and youth use their racial literacies to name when their racialized identities lead to their exclusion or to other violent consequences. Because of systemic racism in schools, and in response to the work that some children, youth, and teachers do to highlight racial literacy and perspectives, we as coaches need to explore our own racial literacies more intentionally. These sorts of literacies are necessary to examine why some diversity is valued and celebrated in schools while other forms are policed.

PAUSE AND REFLECT

How do you model the use of racial literacies for teachers you work with or who you are coaching? How do you center the experiences, through a racial literacy lens, of other educators, community members of children and youth? How do these theories connect with your own definition of justice?

Critical literacies and racial literacies, as a cornerstone of our practice, remind us that we are all full but imperfect and unfinished beings on a quest toward a pluralism of knowing and collective transformation. By separating our archaeology of self, again to draw on Sealey-Ruiz's framework, from the relationships, needs, and desires of the children and families that we serve, we reify traditional schooling patterns and prevent ourselves from experiencing liberation from the oppressive storylines around us. When we are doing design work, we must understand how our biases, identities, and ideologies exist within projects and how they show up in design. They can show up in whose stories are told and who tells them, who benefits from the work, and how laboring for change relates to our institutional, economic, and social histories.

LANGUAGE USE

Let's consider closely what it means to use all the tools we have at hand—tools for making meaning—by examining language. By scrutinizing language, we begin sensitizing ourselves to the diversity and beauty of the world around us. Language is critically important in efforts to move ideas forward into principled action, to create ripples of change, and to resist complacency. In fact, our notion of production places language—including written and spoken language, deep listening, and the creative arts—in the center of the necessary tools for working for justice.

There is another reason we need to pay close attention to language, as language can also operate to disengage and distort efforts toward racial justice in schools. For example, Mica Pollock describes interviews with teachers who mention "problems" or "addressing the issue" or "the special ed kids" (who are primarily Black), among other terms, without naming the racial patterns in discipline or how and why many Black learners are referred to these special services.[11]

These linguistic patterns and the meanings of these words create the storylines that Gee reminds us are so powerful in institutions like schools. The effects of these storylines are pervasive, and as Pollock's learners convey, they often distort how learners *see themselves* (as "disadvantaged youth," "low-tracked," "low-income minority"). We agree with Pollock's findings: when language is used to thrust inequities back on the children and families instead of on the system or systems that perpetuate them, we should be alerted and poised to act.

Language, then, can be a tool for identifying and reconsidering harmful racial patterning in vulnerable or resistant communities. We borrow the term *calling in* from public discourse—in contrast to calling out or simply naming injustices—to describe how we should identify oppressive language or actions while also encouraging reflection and dialogue to build new understandings with our community members.[12] We believe such exchanges matter when people are engaged in design. Here are some examples of how we can use language to call in support and engagement from people in our spheres of influence:

- Call in colleagues, family members, and other stakeholders to examine the use of language to describe learners, their families, and their communities, taking the time to consider how racism or other storylines are evoked with this language.
- Deconstruct language in documents used every day in the settings where we teach and learn, asking similar questions about storylines.
- Retire practices and uses of language that are no longer of service to the community.
- Sit in on meetings of community organizations and observe their language use. Recognize strengths, network with people, and analyze the documents produced by these groups.
- Set aside and honor time to discuss and cowrite agreements for learning together.

- Clearly label the goals of language use that will be used in learning together: *interrupting, calling-in, questioning, reframing,* and *shifting consciousness.*
- Become familiar with disaggregating data for race and ethnicity, especially in any form of assessment or evaluation. Elena Aguilar's equity audit coaching framework provides a good guide.[13]
- Model humility, vulnerability, and apology—and redress in *all* instances of harm.
- Use the arts as a powerful tool to shift awareness.

Contrary to popular agitator belief, it is not always the loudest voice in the room that propels change. Rather, it is the stamina of the whole to persistently engage in actions across spheres of influence. We make sure that a variety of voices have contributed when we use language for production. We must incorporate multiple perspectives, even when these revisions take more time than our systems usually provide. We consider these actions, when they are strung together across time and space, as ripples of change.

Before moving on to the chapters about practical coaching tools, let's look at how spheres of influence and ripples of change relate to coaching. To this end, we'll draw on and extend the ideas of critical and racial literacies and language use to coaching.

COACHING FOR JUSTICE: INITIATING RIPPLES OF CHANGE

Coaching for justice starts with acknowledging oneself, one's communities, the land and spaces occupied by our institutions, and their histories. The health and wellness of all these people and places is both one's responsibility and one's legacy (we return to this idea in chapter 8). Actions are both reciprocal and relational. We must move our coaching beyond own comfort and knowledge to cultivate new knowledge and to activate ripples of change.

What is new about justice-focused coaching? Many models of coaching are centered on equity and justice but overemphasize the expertise of a coach or instructional leader to bring about change. Why is this emphasis a limitation? We have worked in coaching communities long enough to know that instructional leaders and coaches are often brought into systems that prize evaluation and conformity over community-based inquiry. It is part of many systems of schooling to reproduce, rather than question, stable knowledge about teaching and learning. We must instead listen deeply, consider alternative models of practice, and purposefully seek out the stories and lived experiences of our educational colleagues, learners, and families to start ripples of change.[14]

Other models of coaching overemphasize the cycles that are a cornerstone of many programs. Our own teacher education program, led by the state's requirements for field supervision, has often relied on coaching cycles *alone* to develop teaching knowledge. We do see the value in these cycles (see chapter 5), and we suggest revisions to expand and emphasize critical perspectives in these cycles. But coaching cycles will never be enough to create schools where Black, Indigenous, Latinx, multiracial, LGBTQIA+, gender-nonconforming, and differently abled learners thrive and that focus on teaching for justice. We need better tools to identify and disrupt ignorance, fear, and racialized biases.

To reduce transactional methods of instruction and exclusionary practices in the classroom in favor of relational and generative alternatives, we must take great care and time. For educational equity, our coaching must prioritize and create new ways of being, observing, and slowing down. By carefully examining public and private discourses of success, policies, laws, and disaggregated data, we can uncover clues to local inequity. But these clues can also be easy to miss if we do not insist on putting them into dialogue with the experiences and lived knowledge of people across our spheres of influence.

For us as coaches, this work must be intellectual, instructional, and creative. We have to cut the practices and traditions that do not serve our community's coaching needs.

Finally, justice-focused coaching acknowledges the importance of emotion, vulnerability, and empathy in coaching for ripples of change. Cultivating the grace and stamina to learn in public will be physically and emotionally hard. But by stepping out of ourselves (and what we think we know), we can consciously and laboriously position or re-position ourselves as part of a larger collective movement.

As White women, we five have been called out; that is, publicly notified of the ways we use racist, ableist, and other unjust storylines by ourselves and with others. We have also been called *in* to identify, reflect on, and address those injustices when we were perpetuating inequalities in schools. We have been called out and in by colleagues, learners, parents, administrators, and our own loved ones. We have returned to those people in our spheres of influence with vulnerability, knowing that we will certainly make more mistakes. The moments when we have experienced the most painful emotions, when we realize we have made or acted on harmful assumptions about a child or friend, are also those when oppressive storylines of power were operating through us and hurting others. In such cases, humility and empathy go a long way to move us toward reparative action. These experiences of humility and vulnerability—and importantly, the action and changes we have taken because of the care others have shown in guiding our growth toward justice—have influenced the ways we also call in those we mentor as coaches. We call someone in as a continued responsibility to ensure that actions match our collective beliefs in the continual pursuit of justice for learners.

We recognize that power and oppression act on us in various instances, and we use power and oppressive practices both knowingly and unknowingly. These are opportunities to identify and adjust how we show up and react in the future. Instead of calling out people (ourselves included) as needing to be fixed, we consider how to use our critical and racial literacies to disrupt storylines that foster inequity and how to design new ones. And as the work becomes more and more public, we support one another during times of emotional and physical fatigue. We need to put practices in place or develop them across spheres of influence to safely address tensions and snags as they erupt in practice. Because they will.

CONCLUSION

Our research shows that coaching for justice demands responsive and reciprocal engagement with the community of learners and stakeholders across our spheres of influence. We must know what it means to focus locally and how to collaborate across spheres of influence for change. We must also be mindful of how power operates within and across spheres of influence and apply critical and racial literacies and attention to language in our productions. In doing so, we recognize that people across our spheres of influence will want different things. They will interpret our efforts in light of their own prior experiences with education and hold various degrees of institutional power. Some parents, community members, and administrators will want to collaborate, and others will ask us to listen and act on their behalf. As coaches focused on educational equity and justice, we will endeavor to learn about, and learn with, the families and learners who are most marginalized by any given issue. At times we will disappoint certain powerful stakeholders. Consequently, negotiating and revising will become an instrumental tool of our practice, and we must make these processes public, too. We will build dexterity and persistence to address difficult situations, and our coaching will strengthen.

Ripples of change in our coaching practices are just as they sound. Like a pebble in a pond, our practices have impacts that can spread beyond our local spheres. By putting these ideas into action, we link them and, indeed, our own learning toward wider and wider audiences. To be clear, not only do we influence the ripples in our network, but we are also influenced by them. This is the reciprocity and responsibility of collaborating in communities full of diversity and difference.

—— CHAPTER 3 ——

ACTIVELY OBSERVING PRACTICE TOGETHER

Our first coaching tool, described as *actively observing practice together*, puts practice at the center of teacher learning and change. Educators come into the discipline with experiential knowledge, often having spent two decades in schools as a student! What a person can understand about teaching and classroom life as a student or an observer, however, is different from a being in the classroom as a professional who reflects and grows over time. Knowledge grows through practice, but this observation does not necessarily mean that everything is trial and error. Instead, educators use their depth of knowledge as people to understand curricula and their teaching situations and then apply strategies to ensure learning opportunities that are more just. Coaches often enter the journey as partners who, through practice, are also working to adapt and respond to instruction to suit the needs of a diverse group of learners in a classroom. Educators are always on a journey to match values to actions and decision-making, typically by privileging equitable learning opportunities and transformative educational experiences for learners.

When teachers critically observe themselves and others, reflect on what they see, and plan for action, they generate new ways to support the needs of learners and their communities. This type of observation is quite different from the kinds tied to evaluation in many educational contexts. Actively observing practice together, as we will share in this chapter, means aiming for transformation not only in terms of your teaching practices but also importantly for, and with, learners, families, and communities. It is also collaborative across groups that have a diverse set of institutional roles and identities. To actively observe practice together, we must pose challenging questions related to the experiences and observations, even when (especially when!) the questions are uncomfortable. Actively observing practice together is an alternative approach to ensure that our classrooms are more equitable places for learners to thrive.

As a coaching tool, actively observing practice together takes a coach away from the back of the room, where they might be tempted to observe as an objective party. The role of the coach is to guide teachers toward awareness—to facilitate critical reflection of how beliefs and actions align and to bring in perspectives and feedback explicitly from children, youth, family, and the community—and then together move toward action. The coach also engages in reflection and action while serving as a compass to orient the teaching and discussion toward justice and equity in classrooms.

PAUSE AND REFLECT

First, consider your previous experiences with observation (as educators and coaches). What roles did people play during the observation, and what was the focus? Next, consider your previous experiences with observations centered on equity and justice in schools. Have you had these experiences? If not, what got in the way of addressing those issues?

When we as an author team considered the questions posed in the preceding "Pause and Reflect" exercise, we found mixed experiences in our histories around observation. Often, when equity *was* a focus of observing instruction, the coach was seeking out new perspectives to improve practice and experiences for learners. A shortcoming even in our own examples was the lack of engagement of families and community members in our reflections and action plans.

This chapter and chapters 4 through 7 feature templates and questions that help you prepare for and implement a coaching tool. Each of these chapters also includes a case study in which one of us provides a close-up example. In this chapter, you will meet Erica, an instructional literacy coach and school administrator working with Mariana, a bilingual Spanish-English kindergarten teacher.

These five chapters are organized into four sections. The first section presents the theoretical background of the coaching tool; you might think of this background as the theoretical underpinnings of the practical work. In the second section, "Considering Power in Institutional Roles," we speak to the institutional roles that coaches might have and the related affordances and constraints of those roles. We then follow with "A Practical Guide," a step-by-step description of the coaching tool, along with figures and tables to give you concrete ideas of how the tool works. Next, a case study describes the experiences that one or a group of us had, and we end each of these chapters with a few overarching thoughts.

BACKGROUND: WHAT IS ACTIVELY OBSERVING PRACTICE TOGETHER?

Four core ideas serve as background to the coaching tool of actively observing practice together (figure 3.1). A number of researchers have explored these ideas in greater depth; here we offer an introduction to these big ideas.

FIGURE 3.1 *Actively observing practice together: Four core ideas*

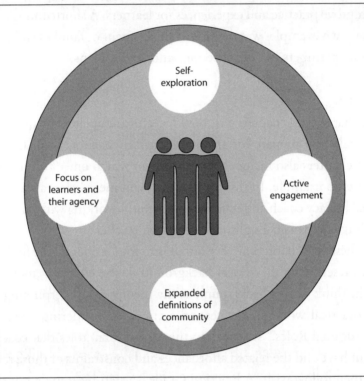

Doing the Groundwork Through an Exploration of Self

Elena Aguilar's model of transformative coaching begins with the self, and she applies her framework to the coach and the individual(s) being coached.[1] Aguilar presents a three Bs framework for coaching: behaviors (skills), beliefs (mental models, knowledge, experiences), and ways of being (emotional intelligence and resilience, disposition, will). She proposes that coaches examine these three Bs within the self and with the person being coached. This examination can also be applied to the larger educational systems and to local classrooms and other environments. We see the connections between this self-examination and Yolanda Sealey-Ruiz's encouragement for racial self-examination, which we explored earlier.[2] To learn with others, in community, toward more just practices in schools, educators and coaches must use lenses of justice and equity to think critically about their ways of being. This work is both individual and collective. Later in this book, we discuss how to do reflective work together in empathy conversations. But for now, we will guide you to reflect on yourself.

HOW CAN WE?   When you want to do this groundwork of attending to your own beliefs, capacities, and skills, the first step is to reflect. You might reflect by drawing, writing, or even recording some thoughts, individually. Table 3.1 offers some questions that you can used for this groundwork.

As discussed earlier, putting ourselves at the center of actively observing practice together runs the risk of reifying individual-centered institutional norms. As you think about starting with the self and the introspective work of defining justice in relation to traditions and cultures in your own spheres of influence, remember that this is just a starting place. Self-examination is hard and always-unfinished work: it includes examining how you teach now and have taught in the past and your values and beliefs. When you do this work beside others in your community, you mitigate the tendency to stay me-focused. Instead, you create opportunities to talk together about the challenge of aligning actions and beliefs, and together you can orient new practices toward justice.

Moving Away from Clipboards and Stools at the Back of the Room

The idea here is to be an active coach. *Active* means being involved in the observation and learning together with teachers. Drawing on Misty Sailors and Logan Manning's scholarship on literacy coaching, an active observer lives as a transformative educator, frequently questioning what they see, in the interest of building new futures with, and for, communities.[3] Each of the critical pedagogical frameworks

TABLE 3.1 *Groundwork: Creating a shared vision for actively observing practice together*

	INDIVIDUAL REFLECTION	COMMUNITY DISCUSSION
Beliefs	What do I believe about equity and justice in education?	What are our shared definitions of equity and justice in education?
Perceived differences	How might my own definitions differ from others in my school or community?	What did we imagine as differences, and did those differences play out the way we imagined?
Examples	What are examples from my own practice I could connect to my definitions? (What do I say and do to orient my teaching toward justice?)	What do we notice about similarities and differences in how we act for justice?
Envisioning	What would it look like and sound like for learners to have opportunities to thrive in classrooms? How might that be unique to the specific grade or content that I teach or observe?	What similarities and differences exist in how we envision justice and equity in the classroom? How might those be related to our different roles and identities?
Resources for learning	How do I already position myself in working for justice with and for the communities I serve?	What resources do we have to draw upon in partnering with communities?
Opportunities for learning	What opportunities do I have as an educator to learn with others in the community about what it means for learners to thrive in schools?	What are our collective visions for partnering more authentically with our communities?

guiding our classroom teaching includes an action component. In culturally sustaining pedagogy, for example, educators are focused on learning about and drawing on learners' lived experiences and knowledge in the classroom. But to be sustaining, a pedagogy must also translate knowledge from the classroom into the outside world and empower learners to transform their schools and other institutions—to increase solidarity and reciprocity.[4]

Actively observing practice together means engaged reflection and action. One mentor teacher described the status quo of observations in their school as "the classic I-sit-in-the-back, you-teach-in-the-front model." We aim to disrupt this default passivity and distant judgment that results when learners sit in the back of the classroom watching the teacher directing the class. When coaches are actively observing practice together, they are a classroom member. The coach interacts in the moment to be a thought partner, to anticipate challenges, or to explore power dynamics and access during the observation. In a later chapter, we will explore this moment-to-moment coaching tool, which we call huddling to confer.

To interact with other educators and learners in the classroom, the active observer frequently spends time in the classroom with an educator either as a coach, co-teacher, or partner. An active observer is one who takes time to arrange how they might engage in an observation. This preparation includes building relationships with a school, a teacher, and learners. An active observer is there in person, participating in a morning meeting or sitting with a small group of learners while they work. This observer could also be watching a recording with another person to coach. For us, the descriptor *active* transforms the coach from an outsider to someone who may be problem-solving, celebrating, asking critical questions of the learners, and collaborating to adapt.

HOW CAN WE? In this chapter, we show you how you can use an observation template to actively observe. Here, we share with you a snapshot of what actively observing practice together looks like and sounds like. As an important starting place, ensure that there are ample opportunities to collaborate so that you can build and explore shared definitions of justice in teaching and in education more broadly. You then continually collaborate on this work throughout subsequent steps in the coaching partnership. First, we recommend a preconference discussion before observing another teacher's practice. Why? You will need a chance to share your definitions and goals and to decide on roles in the observation. These decisions will continually be connected to previously explored definitions and goals of building more just schooling spaces. Second, you need a space to collect snapshots of classroom life. You might prefer a journal or a laptop, but you need a way to capture these observations. Finally, you will need some questions for reflection or discussion. Figure 3.2 is an observation tool template you might use to get started.

Expanding the Definitions of Community

Adding to the theories we've already introduced, Peter Murrell's conception of a community teacher is one who is engaged with systems of schooling and focused on collaboration and inquiry in urban schools.[5] Murrell's seven principles for urban community teachers include attention to both the communities we typically see as guiding teacher learning, such as other educators, administrators, supervisors, and coaches, and the broader circle of families and students. Further, to support all learners, the focus in teacher learning extends from the school to intersections with schooling, including religious and cultural organizations, health care and wellness support, and other systems. The focus is on centering agency, equity, and justice in classrooms and beyond so that learners have experiences that help them to fully thrive. This framework provides an important foundation for how we think about the active role of the coach not only in the classroom but also in community.

In their teaching and research, Mariana Souto-Manning (a university professor) and Jessica Martell (a teacher) explore how families are embraced in the classroom, not as an outside entity.[6] They document a practice of birthday celebrations in Martell's classroom, when family members and other caregivers contribute to a celebration of the child's birthday. In bringing families into the classroom

FIGURE 3.2 *Template observation tool: Actively observing practice together*

Observation date: ___ / ___ / ___	Who is present, and what are their roles?

Mode of observation (circle one): **In Person   Video Recording   Live Video**

Context (circle one): **Co-teaching   Transparent observer   Outside observer**

Preconference discussion (2–3 minutes):
- Have we discussed our shared definitions of equity and justice around this situation?
- Where will each of us be, and what are our roles, during this observation?
- What lenses will we use to focus our observations on issues of justice?

Observational data	**Reflections**
What do you see, and what do you hear? Try to limit your observations to what you can take in with your senses. Avoid interpretations and judgments.	Why did you select these moments? What questions are coming up for you?
Note: Here is where you will jot down your observations. Take as much space as you need.	

Reflection discussion
- Return to your shared definitions and vision of equity and justice.
- What actions were captured in your notes? What was the impact on the learners?
- In light of your discussion, what might be the focus of a future observation?

to celebrate a child, teachers physically locate family members in the classroom as part of classroom life. Families share many of their cultural practices, including but not restricted to celebrations. Many teachers invite family and community members to a closing celebration of a unit to celebrate student work. But what if teachers launched classroom units and other authentic opportunities for families to be highlighted throughout the year? Souto-Manning was not officially Martell's coach, but the professor spent time with Martell actively observing community values by experiencing and documenting the spoken and lived intentions of the community, the learners' sense of curiosity, and their involvement in education. These three observations—community values, curiosity, and involvement—in actively observing practice together are an important part of how coaching prioritizes justice. As teachers and coaches, you cannot expect families to collaborate on understanding and shaping practice unless you are intentional about relationships. As these relationships build, you can invite families in to observe together. Later in this book, we provide a framework for empathy conversations, a tool that you can use to build relationships with families.

Our colleagues Jennifer Adair and Kiyomi Sánchez-Suzuki Colegrove have shown how we can use video to engage various stakeholders, including caregivers, other family members, children, youth, educators, and administrators, in conducting observations with us.[7] Building on Joseph Tobin's foundational research comparing early childhood approaches across cultures, the researchers used what is called video-cued ethnography.[8] Adair and colleagues created videos of classroom practices where learners show agency in their classroom. Focused on young children, the videos disrupt traditional notions of what young children's participation sounds like and looks like in the classroom. After producing the videos, the researchers used them to generate discussion among various stakeholders, such as families, administrators, community members, learners, and teachers. Departing from the traditional uses of video, the video-cued method allowed the researchers to actively observe together with stakeholders who typically are not included in conversations. Although not designed as a coaching tool per se, video-cued ethnography could serve as a tech tool for coaching.

PAUSE AND REFLECT

Do a little imagining and dreaming. What do you think is possible in terms of expanding your communities for actively observing practice together?

Who is part of your larger community in your situation? Which partnerships already exist, and which would you like to strengthen (multidirectionally)? When considering the purpose of actively observing in community, how are you intending to bring in nonhierarchical and multidirectional partnering during the active observation? How do you envision your positioning as a coach? How have you built partnerships with your community in the past? How might those partnerships translate into your using this tool as a coach?

Imagine the possibilities that aren't yet happening in coaching and the school structures or systems that you could build on as a coach. Jot down a few reflections now.

Focusing on the Learners and Their Agency

Aguilar, in *Coaching for Equity*, documents her ongoing relationship with Khai, a kindergarten teacher who asked Aguilar to observe his classroom to understand his struggles with behavior management regarding Jordan, an African American student. Through these active observations, Aguilar gained insight into the ways Khai, who identifies as the child of Vietnamese immigrants, was basing his response to Jordan on his own cultural history of schooling. Over two observations, Aguilar addressed the struggle Jordan faced in a classroom with a teacher who did not imagine a classroom that supports and nurtures him. Aguilar reflects on the high stakes of Khai's punitive interactions that excluded Jordan from the classroom, citing the school-to-prison pipeline as a phenomenon on her mind as a coach. Engaging with active observation, through coaching, Aguilar and Khai eventually reenvisioned the possibilities for Jordan and made actionable plans for subsequent learning and experiences.

Earlier we spoke of the importance of coaches' caring with teachers. When a coach cares with the teacher, they share goals and experiences, and ultimately, the teacher and, most importantly, the children benefit. This means that the coach sees the teacher and children as whole people, as Angela Valenzuela urged in her seminar book about what the Mexican American youth in her study needed from their teachers.[9] Again, as Aguilar posits, every teacher can continue to grow in their practice, and inequities and oppression in schools exist because of structures and institutions. While people can uphold these inequities, the structures and systems are flawed, and thus our coaching must confront this unjust situation. To do so, we must continue our ongoing visits to the classroom, engage with others during and after observations, and reorient the purpose of what it means to be an observer. We need an aligned goal of observing together to move toward justice-oriented instructional practices. This means a shift away from teachers' and coaches' intentions toward an emphasis instead on the impact of how learners are experiencing the lesson and learning.

Hierarchical power relationships around observation are ingrained in our institutions. By observing practice together with other stakeholders, the coach has opportunities to disrupt the expert–novice binaries in coaching practices and can instead prioritize being an engaged learner in a partnership. Recall that central to justice-focused coaching is the disruption of this binary. One way to disrupt the expert–novice divide is to bring more fluidity into the practice, such as taking turns observing one another. Observing together becomes a way to make the invisible decision-making and moment-by-moment interactions in the classroom visible. Unpacking and debriefing lessons together is not about the coach mimicking actions from one teacher to another or asking prescribed reflection questions of the teacher. Instead, actively observing together demands that both teacher and coach examine the rationales behind their practice and analyze not only the how and what of teaching and building relationships but also the why behind instructional and curricular practices. This engaged reflection is key to what we do as co-learners.

Disrupting the expert–novice binary does not stop with coaches and teachers. We recommend emphasizing how actively observing practice together means learning with and from children in the classroom community. This appreciation of children's involvement may be shown in how you model a collaborative, inquiry-based learning approach in the classroom, and how you reflect on your own practice during and after an observation. We are not only asking ourselves how we feel the lesson went or was perceived but also making sure that we have learned with and from children about what they actually experienced, appreciated, or found relevant in the lesson observed together. By encouraging mentees to engage with children during their time in the classroom, the coach offers an active and reflective positioning of the value of all the voices in the community, and most importantly, the coach prioritizes the impact of the lesson over the intent of the teacher.

HOW CAN WE? Table 3.2, on the next page, offers some questions to consider in relation to student agency and practice in the classroom.

POWER IN INSTITUTIONAL ROLES

People in different coaching roles will uniquely hold power and have responsibility for both the teachers they collaborate with and others such as administrators. These many responsibilities come with challenges. For example, consider a coach who is committed to justice-focused coaching by supporting their colleagues and upholding

TABLE 3.2 *Groundwork: Guiding questions for actively observing community values*

Learner agency	How are the learners positioned in the classroom? For example, are they leaders, designers, passive receivers, or something else? How do you know? What examples can you provide?
Teacher responsiveness	How does the teacher facilitate the lesson or learning experience so that it evolves in response to the learners? How are learners engaged in the lesson? What examples might show this?
Learner interaction	How do learners learn together in a community? How do they relate to and position each other? For example, are they competitors, co-learners, helpers, allies, or something else? What evidence shows this?
Belonging	Is each child seen, valued, and respected? How do you know? What aspects of identity are the safest and most valued in this space? The least valued? The least safe?

and working within the system and school expectations. Coaches, together with educators, can build a practice of observing, talking about decision-making, linking actions to beliefs, and dreaming of new possibilities. This ongoing conversation may take different forms throughout a school year or over a longer period. Such an ongoing conversation can serve as a foundation for the predictable, mandatory, and high-stakes formal observations or evaluations that sometimes are part of institutions. For coaches, these ongoing conversations require vulnerability and transparency to learn with and alongside those they are coaching and reorienting their own observations toward justice-oriented conversations and transformation in classrooms.

Here and in other discussions of coaching tools, we offer a few "How Can We?" scenarios to invite you and your community to think about these dynamics in your setting and in the local community. For actively observing practice together, we envision the dual roles of a collaborative and critical coach and someone who may also have to evaluate others. Another challenge might be the need to navigate as an outsider, such as in a field supervisor role. As an outsider, you may not yet have strong relationships with the adults in the school building or local community or with the children.

How can coaches actively observe together when they are also in positions that require them to formally evaluate teachers? Here are two suggestions:

1. Engage in open and transparent conversations with the coaching community. You can talk about this conflict, ensure that there is clarity on when the evaluations versus collaborative coaching will occur, and identify the similarities in, and differences between, the shared coaching experiences and the more evaluative roles.

2. Engage in frequent post-experience reflections together, asking questions such as these: How did this experience feel? What worked for you, and how might I better support you?

How can educators actively observe together when the coach is seen as an outsider to the school and classroom community?

- If you are seen as an outsider, add more face time together either inside or out of the classroom to build a relationship when possible. If face time is not feasible, have a transparent discussion of what the teacher needs for a trusting environment, and follow those leads when using this tool and beyond.
- We also recommend embracing your vulnerability to model and share your own reflections of your teaching practices (present or past) and keeping your vulnerability embedded in this tool to foster a sense of shared journey toward more just teaching and learning.

These are some of the many power dynamics and responsibilities that might impinge on this coaching tool in a school setting. Most importantly, we recommend having transparent discussions about these dynamics and responsibilities, seeking out shared mitigation actions together, and revisiting your decisions and actions throughout your time together. Building trust comes from the work that you engage in, and that work includes this coaching tool. Your goal is to ensure that power dynamics and your responsibilities as a coach are not overlooked when you apply this coaching tool and others.

ACTIVELY OBSERVING PRACTICE TOGETHER: A PRACTICAL GUIDE

Now that we have provided some background and ideas on actively observing practice together, we want to help you as a teacher or coach implement this tool. What follows is a step-by-step practical guide for your decision-making.

Step 1. Make Time for Journaling and Shared Justice Orientations

As we discussed earlier, you'll want to set aside some time to reflect on your own justice orientations and those you share with the teachers or coaches you'll be observing practice with. For example, with others, you might decide to set aside forty minutes, for four consecutive weeks, to prepare for actively observing practice together. The sequence of tasks might follow this order:

1. *Personal writing time:* Use this time for private journaling (see table 3.1).
2. *Sharing your writing:* Each person has an opportunity to share.
3. *Discussion on the similarities and differences between your ideas and responses to the questions:* In this part of the process, we encourage you to share how your teaching decisions influence learners. The idea is to begin moving in a synchronized manner with others. A synchronized focus does not mean

identical approaches to teaching and learning but instead means an aligned vision of what justice-oriented instruction might entail in the focal classroom spaces. Having different perspectives, different teaching styles, but a shared approach to equity and justice in the classroom allows for a collaborative environment where you can engage in actively observing (and acting on it together). These conversations will serve as an anchor for your observations together.

4. *Planning for actively observing practice together:* Here are three possibilities for this step. First, teachers in a co-teaching environment can actively observe community values. Second, a coach can observe teachers' practices transparently to model actively observing practice together. Finally, coaches can use active observation of community values as a tool when they are positioned as an outside observer. Before beginning their observations, a group might decide to follow all three approaches or implement only one or a few of them. The choices will differ according to circumstances.

Step 2. Conduct the Observation

For the template in figure 3.2, you have the three possibilities described in step 4. The template is an observation protocol, not a rubric or a checklist. It is a tool for you to document your observations: What do you see? What do you hear? In the "Observational data" block, try to limit your observations to what you can take in with your senses, and avoid interpretations and judgments. After collecting this data, you will use the "Reflection" block to connect what you see, hear, and notice with your thoughts on the why of those observations. This step is essential as it allows you to decide on where you think beliefs should connect to actions and instructional moves in the classrooms. It is the precursor to deepening practices toward justice.

HOW DO WE ACTIVELY OBSERVE WHEN CO-TEACHING?   When using this protocol during co-teaching, begin with the preparation questions in table 3.1, and find some time to discuss them together to share your
justice orientations. You might also use this time to ask one another,
How are we physically (or digitally) positioned in the classroom to
take an active role as teachers and observers? Where will we be situated? How might that feel for learners? If you anticipate that having
two people doing the same thing may add unwanted power dynamics to the classroom, you should consider how to mitigate these challenges. You might even consider video recording and watching the
videos together afterward, until you establish a way of working collaboratively in the space.

You may want to quickly check in before teaching, asking, What
in this specific lesson would show that learners have opportunities to
thrive? How can we ensure that we are having opportunities as observers, coaches, or teachers, and are these opportunities bidirectional?
Will we take turns to start? During teaching, you might choose to
sit side by side to attend to the learners in the classroom, rather than
observing from the back of the room.

The template can be something that both teachers hold in front
of them on a clipboard and on which they jot down notes when the
other person is speaking. We also recommend making opportunities to huddle, or have quick conferences (see chapter 4), to debrief
in-the-moment decisions. We will not go into detail about huddles
here, but we suggest these as opportunities to notice and name what
the other person is doing, to ask a question, or to disrupt inequities
when you see them occurring.

After an observation, we encourage you to return to your shared
definitions of equity and justice and visions of what it looks like to
engage in equitable practices. Debriefing the observations, you might
shift from the left-hand block to the right-hand one in figure 3.2,
asking one another to reflect on the purposes and outcomes of the

actions. Together, you might reflect on how, overall, you know the lesson was transformative (or not) for students, and what evidence each person wrote down about what happened and why. At the bottom of the template, you can make some space to keep track of your discussion.

HOW DO WE OBSERVE OURSELVES TRANSPARENTLY WITH OTHERS?   Coaches will often decide to put themselves out there, teaching and allowing themselves to be actively observed. As a coach, you can use the template we provided in figure 3.2 for actively observing practice together to model observation practices. Coaches can use live teaching or videos of their own teaching to model these practices. We've found it is most helpful to use everyday examples and practice analyzing teaching decisions toward justice-oriented instruction. Video allows you to rewatch and revisit your instructional decisions shortly after your teaching or coaching. We encourage you to take coaching stances similar to those you would take with others to examine asset-based moves, inquire into practice, and make decisions from student-centered lenses. Asking the question How am I providing opportunities for each child to thrive each minute of the lesson? sets a high bar. It requires constant framing and reframing while you decenter yourself as the teacher, and it requires prioritizing responsive, strengths-based, and culturally sustaining instructional practices. This practice can then be one that the teachers you coach can add to their tool kits.

As a coach, you might start reflection and debriefing with some time away, writing and thinking about how you opened your practice and reflections to others. You can then reflect on how you engaged the teachers you were coaching in their practice and reflection. Another question to reflect on is this: what alternatives were you and the observers able to identify for instruction, and perhaps most importantly, what was the impact of the process on learners? You will be continuously revisiting your stance toward justice and evaluating the impact of your coaching on learners. Together with the teachers who were part of the observation process, you might also debrief with one another, reflecting on how the process went and identifying the next steps. Is there another opportunity for you to be observed and to model reflection on your teaching? Will you now move to observing the teacher? And what might go differently if the roles were switched?

HOW DO WE OBSERVE ACTIVELY AS AN OUTSIDER?   Perhaps most commonly as a coach, you might be in a situation to observe others as an outsider to the practice. In this case, we recommend first engaging in observing yourself transparently with teachers to build trust. Evaluate your relationship with the teacher or teachers you are working with, and determine how comfortable they will be with your observation. Can you start with another option for observation if you're not sure?

Another consideration is what it means to gain access to the setting. Active observation means that even if you are an outsider to the setting, you will need to gain access and trust with the learners as well as the teacher. This might mean joining a community-building circle with the class to experience the classroom from the learners' perspectives and practices. Or it might entail asking learners about their experiences and opportunities to engage as learners to be in and with the community.

We encourage an awareness of how and where you physically sit or stand in the classroom, your body language, and how you are intending to interact with learners and the teacher. How do you focus on being involved and gathering information during your observation so that you can use a justice lens? One way is to ask questions about power, positioning, engagement, community, and choice in the classroom. Revisit figure 3.2 and table 3.2 for question suggestions. Reflect on these questions and note any evidence you have collected that informs your thinking about your answers.

Step 3. Expand the Shared Observing
Approach to the Larger Community

To actively observe practice together, we also need a way to bring in perspectives from learners and community members. While learners and community members may not weigh in on every observation, we need partnerships with children and families when trying to make schools more equitable and just. What does it look like and sound like to expand actively observing practice together to the larger community? We encourage pathways that allow for authentic feedback and reflection with caregivers and adults beyond the walls of the school community. This means creating opportunities to have conversations about teaching practices and learning experiences at home. In this regard, the learning, discussion, and active observing is shared—not simply an invitation from school to homes, but a partnership.

Here are a few practical tools for actively observing practice together with family and community members. First, you could invite families into the classroom to be observers. Imagine you are teaching a unit that focuses on home and out-of-school literacies. Family members might actively observe during a classroom activity to think with you about how students can use their knowledge and experience in the unit. This approach disrupts traditional expert–novice distinctions to position family members as coaches. What do you imagine they would see happening in the classroom, and how might they coach you to be more responsive to the learners?

Using table 3.1 as a guide (see page 50), you might explicitly ask people to observe the action in the classroom, and then afterward have an opportunity to debrief their observations. You might ask them to tell you what they saw and otherwise noticed, and what they wondered about their observations. The purpose of including family members in active observation is to open your classroom in ways that disrupt traditional parent involvement, which often positions parents as helpers. In this activity, parents are asked to be thought partners in exploring critical questions about how children are provided agency, choice, and opportunities to share and build on their knowledge; about how they form relationships with others; or about other goals of the community.

In the following case study, one of us (Erica) shares her story about her experience of actively observing practice together with Mariana, a teacher she was coaching, as a justice-focused coaching tool.

ERICA AND MARIANA'S STORY

In her first year as a bilingual instructional coach, Erica had the tremendous opportunity to work with Mariana, a bilingual first-year kindergarten teacher. Situated in a two-way dual-language learning environment, justice orientations were central in ensuring that linguistic capital was privileged in each lesson and learning opportunity. As an emergent bilingual coach working with a skilled and compassionate bilingual teacher, Erica found that actively observing practice together was an opportunity to prioritize Mariana's goals and to explore and amplify her strengths as a teacher. Mariana was especially skilled at integrating children's interests and their literacy and linguistic strengths into her whole- and small-group lessons. However, she hoped to offer more choice and agency in the learning experiences.

First, Erica reflected on her own choices as a coach in terms of how to approach actively observing practice together. She considered the benefit of sharing video recordings of her own teaching, as she was teaching one section of the kindergarten literacy classes each day. However, because of scheduling constraints, she decided to support Mariana with setting goals together and reflecting on practice as a model. Given that Erica also taught the same kindergarten students once a week, the two women were able to work together to imagine how to provide authentic choices for students. As a coach, Erica learned alongside Mariana because they had examined their shared and different experiences. In retrospect, Erica believes she may have missed an opportunity to observe together as co-teachers, because of her choices as a coach.

Step 1. Reflect on and Create Shared Justice Orientations

Early in their partnership, the two of them had conversations that helped Erica understand Mariana's goals as a teacher and the areas she was most focused on in her instruction. For example, the new teacher wanted to offer the children more agency and choice during her literacy lessons. The women's conversations were informal and broad, creating an opportunity for Erica as the coach to understand Mariana's vision for fostering a bilingual and bicultural classroom community for the children she was teaching. They discussed the challenges of finding quality Spanish children's literature in the local library, and they gradually generated book lists. In their partnership, it became clear that they shared many of the same values regarding instructional practices, namely, a focus on a community that provided choice, challenge, agency, and care. But recognizing that Mariana often second-guessed her decisions as a first-year teacher, Erica wanted to amplify her tremendous teaching. This meant disrupting the expert–novice dichotomy and instead exploring the first-year teacher's practice with her, aiming together to match her actions to her visions as a teacher, and sharing Erica's own continuous learning as an educator. The coach's role was to use the tool of actively observing practice together as a spotlight for Mariana to zoom into moments and for both women to pose problems and solve them together as educators.

They started with conversations about ideal classroom communities and learning contexts, Mariana's goals for her teaching, and where she thought her teaching could align with these goals. She envisioned a classroom that valued and embraced the children's funds of knowledge and linguistic capital while also ensuring that behavioral needs were met with care and compassion. Their collaborative practice grew over time through continual dialogue. As the coach, Erica openly talked about her own experiences and goals as an educator, but her aim was to foster a shared vision and to show her vulnerability in how she was continually addressing her own instruction and coaching as well. Erica and Mariana met formally at least once a week and had frequent informal conversations and check-ins to maintain an ongoing discussion about what was working, how Mariana was providing opportunities for children to thrive, and areas for which she wanted continued sharing ideas and support. Because they were in frequent contact (through email, sharing videos, sticky notes, texts, etc.), hard conversations came easily. Actively observing practice together seemed to provide space for vulnerability that a coaching cycle may not have provided.

Step 2. Actively Observe Practice Together

Erica taught Mariana's kindergarten class once a week for an additional literacy- and community-focused special course. In this way, she got to know the children and could share her own experiences of teaching and learning with the class community. In discussions with Mariana, she often related anecdotes from her own instruction and discussed how she shared, and was continuing to uphold, Mariana's vision of prioritizing children's agency and autonomy in learning and how she was considering adjusting in the future. This was a small part of their coaching conversations but an important one that allowed the coach to be fully present in the classroom, to know Mariana as a teacher, and to know the children, their interests (and disinterests), strengths, and habits as learners and people. Erica's situation is probably not the same for all coaches, but finding opportunities to get to know the children and the class community is an essential part of being an active observer with the teacher and children.

Mariana and Erica had a strong relationship, and the first-year teacher frequently asked her coach to stop by for a learning experience or to sit with a child during a challenging time. If Erica was unavailable, Mariana had an iPad ready to capture a video so that they could actively observe together retroactively. This interaction happened regularly throughout the year, and Erica often sat with children at tables or on the carpet or even taught and learned one-on-one or in small groups with children at the teacher's request. In this way, Mariana could capture what the children were doing and saying, and Erica could chat with her during and after teaching and actively observing together as appropriate about their observations on access, choice, agency, and community.

Both women primarily focused on actively observing practice together through video. Because of the fast-paced nature of a kindergarten classroom, video recording allowed them to sit side by side and observe the learning experiences together. However, unlike how a formal observation is conducted, they also used video to slow down the experiences and be thought partners and problem solvers, capturing thoughts about Mariana's instruction and the impact on children's learning. The shared observation was a tool to continually review beliefs about children, bilingualism, and biculturalism in her instructional practices. Mariana and Erica explored different places to set the video camera to capture various perspectives in the classroom and rewatched some moments to continue to facilitate their dialogue about the instruction and the children's learning. Most important, their discussions and the use of video allowed both Mariana and Erica to capture their observations of the children from different perspectives.

Step 3. Expand Actively Observing Together to Larger Communities

Even if the coaching dialogue is rich, as coaches, we must continue to consider spheres of influence. We might adjust or expand our actions outside of the classroom to create more just and equitable learning experiences for learners in the classroom. Mariana was an outstanding teacher already striving to offer opportunities for children to thrive as learners and people in her Spanish kindergarten classroom. However, together she and Erica were able to identify her teaching practices that helped children use these opportunities. The women also looked closely at her language and focused in on individual children who Mariana identified as not having their needs fully met in the classroom.

Erica also used actively observing practice together an additional way: while the teacher taught, Erica would individually talk with children about what would support them so that they would thrive in the classroom. When the two women came back together, they discussed what the coach had learned, to plan for future instruction. Their active observations became a catalyst for discussions, for planning future observations, and, importantly, for planning collaborative work with the children.

Some of the observations that Marian and Erica made are shown in figure 3.3. The notes represent a small part of the conversation and coaching tool of actively observing practice together. During the larger conversation, Mariana and Erica explored what the teacher's goals were in the classroom. For example, one goal was to encourage the children's pride in their bilingualism and their confidence as readers. In the figure, you see Mariana's reflections on the dynamics of the groups and her desire to ensure access for each child. Erica's reflective questions generally supported a continued expansion in the ongoing conversation about Mariana's teaching and development. During these observations Erica often sat with Mariana and the reading group on the floor, other small groups in the classroom, or checked in on learners at Mariana's request.

Roles, Responsibilities, and Power in This Story

Erica and Mariana faced the first power dynamic mentioned earlier in the chapter—the conflict inherent in the collaborative and evaluative responsibilities if you are a coach. As a school administrator, Erica was not only an informal coach for Mariana but also an evaluator.

FIGURE 3.3 *Applied observation tool: An example of actively observing practice together*

Observation date: 03/03/20	Who is present, and what are their roles? *Erica (Administrator)* *Mariana (Teacher)* *Watched recorded lesson together*

Mode of observation (circle one): **In Person (Video Recording) Live Video**	
Context (circle one): **Co-teaching (Transparent observer) Outside observer**	

Preconference discussion (2–3 minutes):
- Have we discussed our shared definitions of equity and justice around this situation?
- Where will each of us be, and what are our roles, during this observation?
- What lenses will we use to focus our observations on issues of justice?

Observational data	Reflections
What do you see, and what do you hear? Try to limit your observations to what you can take in with your senses. Avoid interpretations and judgments.	Why did you select these moments? What questions are coming up for you?
Mariana *I was teaching guided reading. I had four students near me to practice new strategies. . . . The rest of the class was engaged with their own books. . . .* *I was focused on helping one child to engage with the other peers in the group, and another child to feel successful as a reader. They both often shut down or try to leave the group.*	**Mariana** *The group got a little off track at the end. I tried new strategies in my teaching and tried to reorganize how we met and how they would share what they were doing as readers. . . .*
Erica *I noticed that you were working with a small group, and they were sitting in self-selected seats on the floor near you. You had a variety of texts and tools for them to use and had changed the groups to be skills based.*	**Erica** *How did you decide to switch to a skills-based group (from the leveled groups you tried before)? Also, I'm curious about the children selecting their texts. Was this to provide more autonomy?*

continues

FIGURE 3.3 *Continued*

Erica (*continued*)	Erica (*continued*)
I noticed you offered more space for children to share their ideas with each other by writing or drawing on sticky notes or by speaking aloud to you. This seems like a new approach. I also noticed that you took a facilita-tor role rather than a director role, and each child . . .	*I'm wondering if you were able to ask the kiddos what worked for them about some of the adjustments.*

Reflection discussion
• Return to your shared definitions and vision of equity and justice.
• What actions were captured in your notes? What was the impact on the learners?
• In light of your discussion, what might be the focus of a future observation?

There was a natural tension in that many of the observations were often used for the evaluations. While the evidence from these obser-vations was often an asset that highlighted Mariana's strengths, we recognize that the evidence is not always so complimentary in these dynamics as teachers and coaches wrestle with coaching and teaching in justice-oriented perspectives. As suggested earlier, Erica and Mar-iana had explicit conversations about these roles, and the frequency with which they collaborated in coaching models mitigated the weight of the evaluative roles. However, evaluation still often overshadowed the collaborative view, and from a systemic perspective, part of this work is to extend the spheres of influence beyond our local control. We encourage you in your communities to scrutinize what is evalu-ated and how it reflects your shared vision for justice in teaching and learning in schools. We problematize that observation checklists are adequate for meeting the needs of classrooms where children thrive. We need to navigate power, address it, and try to redistribute it in our shared understanding of how we observe, how we are positioned when we are observing, and how we talk about the other expectations that affect our roles as coaches.

CONCLUSION

In this chapter, we expand the approach of actively observing practice together as a justice-focused coaching tool. For educators, this tool is an engaged experience for partners or groups and is less formal than a traditional observation cycle. It is an opportunity for educators and coaches to explore different realities of teaching and begin to see practice more fully. The idea of actively observing practice together also emphasizes the *action* associated with justice; together, coaching teams continually align the activities in the classroom to their visions of justice in teaching and learning.

A coach has various ways to engage in this tool, but they all involve a level of critical self-reflection, vulnerability, humility, and facilitation. The coach serves as a compass for the discussion and observations to ensure that the shared work aligns with a collaborative understanding of equity and justice in teaching and learning and that action results from the shared observation. Actively observing practice together is also a tool for building strong partnerships as coaches and teachers aligning their beliefs and actions toward justice. By finding opportunities for formal and informal, scheduled and unscheduled collaborative learning, coaches and teachers can together promote the value and impact of this tool.

—— CHAPTER 4 ——

HUDDLING TO CONFER

Building on the previous tool of actively observing practice together, in this chapter, we propose huddling to confer as a coaching move to be used *during* observations—to pause the flurry of action that occurs in a classroom setting. In a huddle, the coach and the teacher do a quick analysis of the situation, make decisions, and together plan for action. Huddling expands on our double meaning of justice-focused coaching by disrupting expert–novice divides and expanding how we coach in community.

As literacy scholars, we believe that the notion of huddling has direct connections to the classroom practice of teachers conferring with students as an instructional approach. Carl Anderson describes these conferences as a "conversation," explaining the importance of the following elements of a conversation: making eye contact, talking as readers or writers, and actively listening.[1] Conferring focuses on the work the student is doing as a reader or writer. Conferring acts as a springboard for the teacher be in conversation with the student where both parties can probe and question the work. Because the reader or writer might disagree with the teacher's nudge and might keep on their previous path, the literacy conference recognizes the humanity of the person being coached as well as their agency.[2] Throughout this chapter, we develop huddling to confer as an informal and active coaching tool for justice-focused coaching.

Hereafter we will call this tool *huddling* for clarity but will distinguish *huddling to confer* from previous versions that are specific to co-teaching.[3] An instructional coach sitting in the back of the class and waiting for the lesson to end before they can provide feedback will not be able to huddle. Huddling is dynamic and happens live and during the action. It makes the invisible actions or interactions in a classroom community visible by empowering teachers to reflect on the teaching decisions they make every moment. Huddling can also provide coaches and teachers with an opportunity to identify and question the injustices they observe during the everyday interactions in the classroom.

PAUSE AND REFLECT

Take a moment to consider what already feels accessible about this coaching tool. Many teachers we have worked with and who are mentoring or coaching other teachers have told us that huddling feels quite normal as a coaching tool. What have your experiences been with this kind of spontaneous coaching? What might be some of the benefits of this coaching tool? What do you anticipate might be some of the challenges?

This chapter will follow the same structure as chapter 3, with both background and practical tools for using huddling as a coaching tool. You'll hear a story from one of us (Claire) later in the chapter. She'll describe her use of huddling in a virtual environment as a field supervisor in a teacher education program for secondary school English teachers in an urban area.[4]

BACKGROUND: WHAT IS HUDDLING TO CONFER?

Throughout this section, we will draw your attention to big ideas related to huddling. We will introduce you to some researchers who have informed our thinking about huddling and some practical tools for getting started in your own coaching partnerships.

Exploring Justice Through Puzzling Moments

Huddling comes from the work of Elizabeth Soslau and her colleagues at the University of Delaware.[5] In their teacher preparation program, they encourage co-teaching between student teachers and their mentors. Both co-teachers experience the same events unfolding in the classroom, but huddling allows for one of teachers to initiate an "impromptu sidebar" to examine an event and adapt in the moment.[6] Building on their scholarship, we have chosen to expand huddling because it is often used in co-teaching between a clinical teacher and mentor.

We also draw on the work of Cynthia Ballenger, who focuses on puzzling moments that occur in the classroom when the teacher does not know either what exactly the student knows or what they are working on, but the teacher is curious to learn more.[7] Akin to a teachable moment or an opportunity to address a tension in learning, huddling creates space for a coach to home in on these puzzling moments and embrace the tension. Puzzling moments are opportunities to identify and question the injustices teachers see as they observe the everyday interactions in the classroom. Teachers witness micro- and macro-injustices all the time. The fear is that without guidance or support from a coach on how to intervene after witnessing an injustice, a teacher might be paralyzed by not knowing how to handle it, and the event goes unaddressed. Justice-focused coaching helps teachers facing this sort of challenge by opening a channel of dialogue in the form of a huddle. The huddle is an entry point of inquiry where both the teacher and the coach can ask questions about classroom dynamics that might be hiding or disguising injustices.

If you picture yourself co-teaching or actively observing practice together, you can imagine a moment when you might need to make a decision. Here are a few examples:

- You notice that a child who identifies as nonbinary is misgendered by another student. You know you need to pause the action but are not exactly sure whether to address the child who was misgendered privately or publicly.[8]
- The students are still deeply engaged in a group mathematics problem, but the time is up and you need to make the transition to science. Do you keep working or ask the students to clean up their manipulatives?
- The student teacher in your classroom has planned a brain break, and you notice that the activity requires physical activity. You realize that the brain break will not be accessible to all learners; some students will be unable to perform that action. Do you allow the activity to continue or pause the action to replan the activity in the moment?

There is no straightforward path in each of these scenarios—it is up to the teachers in the classroom to quickly check in on their reactions and their justice orientations to make a snap decision. This idea of a puzzling moment is very important to our conception of huddling and can be helpful for a newer teacher because they are still learning how to respond to certain situations in the classroom.

In figure 4.1, we share how huddling is a modification of the framework for actively observing practice together. The teacher or the observer uses this tool to record a puzzling moment, noting what happens when the action is paused. With this method, as a coach or an observer, you can distinguish a huddle from your other observation notes.

Huddling offers flexibility on who initiates the conversation around a puzzling moment. When huddling, the teacher can notice

FIGURE 4.1 *Template observation tool: Huddling to confer*

Observation date: ___ / ___ / ___	Who is present, and what are their roles?

Mode of observation (circle one): **In Person** **Live Video**

Context (circle one): **Co-teaching** **Transparent observer** **Outside observer**

Observational data	Reflections
What did you observe happening in the classroom?	This is a space for you as the coach to record your thinking around the huddle. What does this moment reveal? What new questions are formed?
Huddle 1 • Who or what initiated the huddle? • What is the purpose of the huddle: To wonder about, affirm, or disrupt something? • What did it sound like? • What happened next?	
Huddle 2 (time) • Who or what initiated the huddle? • What is the purpose of the huddle: To wonder about, affirm, or disrupt something? • What did it sound like? • What happened next?	

an event in the class, quickly debrief with the coach, and then adjust accordingly. In this way, the teacher can take ownership of the inquiry into their teaching by initiating the conversation with their coach instead of waiting to be the recipient of feedback after the lesson has ended. These huddling conversations thus become a channel of dialogue between the coach and the teacher. The conversations place both parties on an equal playing field, despite structural expectations that might perpetuate power hierarchies. This fluid idea of huddling fosters awareness within the lesson, allowing the barriers between expert and novice to come down.

Safety: The Foundation of Successful Huddling

Like other coaching approaches, huddling works best when it happens in a trusting relationship built on ongoing dialogue and continued collaboration. Elena Aguilar writes that trust is how coaches "create the safety . . . that allows beliefs to change."[9] This safety strengthens trust through conversations that she describes as the "bridges needed to be trustworthy." Trust through dialogue is especially important if the huddle is aimed at interrupting inequitable practices in the classroom, especially if there is a room full of learners eager to learn.

For the huddle to not feel like an interruption of the classroom flow, the relationship between coach and teacher must have a foundation of trust that often builds when both parties know each other's expectations. As we suggest later, empathy conversations are one way to develop relationships that have this kind of trust. While huddling is usually quick, it is a part of the larger and ongoing conversation that happens between two people who are working together on their teaching. When teachers have done this work to know one another, they are better equipped to quickly check in to make one of the countless decisions that teachers make every hour.

PAUSE AND REFLECT

You might return to the groundwork for actively observing practice together (table 3.1) before beginning a huddle. How have you worked to create trust with the individuals you coach? What are some practices that you might want to try, to strengthen the coaching relationship?

Building a relationship of trust can take time, especially if coaching has previously been associated with evaluations or high stress for a person in the relationship. Justice-focused huddling is an opportunity to disrupt normativity and turn the attention away from standardized evaluations and instead look to the teacher and the learners themselves and the goals they have for their work.

We have noticed, however, that some people, especially those who are less adept or used to naming injustices in the classroom, may have fears of sounding racist or may feeling inadequate or unready to discuss injustices. However, if we back away from these conversations because of such fears, we protect only the very systems we are trying to shift. Coaching without risk cannot disrupt injustices, especially for those who have endured historical, racialized traumas of schooling writ large.

Huddling Is Intentional

Although this coaching tool is responsive and nimble, it is also intentional. Teachers confer for a purpose. Huddling is not merely a check-in about what time the assembly is after lunch. It is more deeply rooted in bringing to light class events that might be missed with one set of eyes. Huddling expands the second aim of justice-focused coaching as well. It focuses on generative moments, those that lead to new knowledges and inquiries. Specifically, huddles enable us to connect with the communities we serve and to place justice back at the center of coaching.

Coaches and teachers use huddling for three intentions (figure 4.2). Let's look at them in more detail now.

AFFIRMATION. During coaching, an affirmation serves to notice and name a teaching action that is positive. A coach might use an affirmation when they want to point out something that the teacher did and that would be useful to continue to use in similar situations. When teachers are so engrossed in the act of teaching, they can have difficulty seeing

FIGURE 4.2 *The three intentions behind huddling to confer*

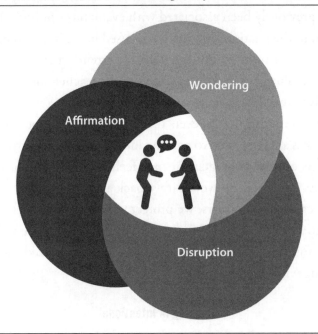

what is happening in a lesson, let alone what is going well. Huddling to affirm allows another person to shed light on a moment or an action and thus encourages the teacher to continue. In justice-focused coaching, affirmations might be limited to the teaching practices that demonstrate alignment of beliefs and actions. Coaches might focus on the teaching moves that reflect the community's justice orientations, such as anti-racist teaching, critical literacies, or promoting student inquiry and agency. Affirmations foster relationship building as well. Through affirmations, we show one another that our orientations toward justice are shared and that we have witnessed one another's efforts toward changing our practice in those directions. Especially given that some coaching relationships have historically been steeped in evaluations and one-sided feedback, huddling to affirm intentionally sheds light on the humanizing possibilities of coaching.

Affirmations could be extended to students and communities. When we affirm a student's strength, we note how the learner is responding to the planned activities or the language of the teacher. For example, a coach might say to a teacher, "When you checked for understanding, we saw that Stefan had a pretty deep understanding of the concept you were teaching about. I wonder what else we can learn about what he has learned from working with his grandmother in the garden." Affirmations, then, move to what we can learn and be amazed about when it comes to what learners know and can do.

WONDERING.   As huddling to affirm focuses on the strengths of the teacher and students, huddling to wonder cultivates a curiosity in the teacher by asking questions of their own practice. When huddling to wonder, the teacher or instructional coach can pose a question and receive a response. The teacher can then immediately try it out in the classroom, growing the muscle of receiving feedback and enacting change. For example, a teacher might say to the instructional coach, "It seems as if Drew is the only one participating. I wonder how I can engage more learners without dismissing Drew." and the instructional coach could offer a suggestion for the teacher to try. Therefore, wondering is an invitation that can continue to build a relationship and practice of shared inquiry that we will return to later in the book.

The invitation to wonder is another entry point for justice-focused coaching because of the in situ nature of the invitation. For example, a wonder huddle might interrupt a racist or homophobic comment that a learner makes during a classroom conversation. Imagine a coach asking, "I wonder what storylines the learner is drawing on in this comment and how we might learn more about where his comment is coming from." With guidance and the appropriate language, teachers learn how to address these instances with care and curiosity rather than with fear of making a mistake by saying the wrong thing. Returning to ripples of change, we imagine the invitation to wonder as an approach that gives teachers and coaches power beyond the classroom as lifelong learners; through wondering, they also develop practices of curiosity and inquiry to pursue justice.

DISRUPTION.   When we confer to disrupt an action, we are typically noticing an injustice that relates to a question we share, such as how racism is affecting the learners in the classroom. When huddling to disrupt, the teacher, serving as a coach in the moment, pauses to quickly analyze the classroom to identify an injustice and step in to disrupt what is happening.

For example, in one of our research studies on huddling, a cooperating teacher, who was White and identified as an anti-racist educator, shared with us that during an observation, she heard a teacher candidate who was reading a Langston Hughes poem repeatedly use the word *colored* to describe Black people in the analysis of the poem. Hughes used the word *colored* in the poem, but the teacher candidate was using the word without framing it in a historical context. She may have never had a conversation about the word, and we believe she may have conflated the term with *person of Color*, a common term in this classroom's discourse. The teacher candidate was Asian American and did not share a history with the author of this poem, and the cooperating teacher knew that she was not accustomed to talking with a multiracial group of learners about race. The cooperating teacher made a decision to huddle with the teacher candidate when the children turned to talk about the poem. The cooperating teacher used the space created by the huddle to discuss with the teacher candidate her use of the word *colored*.

In the huddle, the cooperating teacher said to her, "I noticed you have been saying 'colored people' because it was a line in the poem, but now that you are discussing the characters in the poem, it should be 'people of Color.'" Instead of having the preservice teacher continue using *colored* for the duration of the class, the cooperating teacher took the opportunity to huddle to confer in the moment, which allowed the preservice teacher to act immediately. There was little time to talk about the historical context, but later, they were able to debrief and unpack what happened.

Because huddling is an in-the-moment coaching tool, we need to recognize how Whiteness, ableism, and other dominant perspectives shape our coaching and how we learn from those influences. By being aware of how some teachers may react to huddling in certain situations, we uncover clues to areas of collaborative growth. For example, many White teachers may struggle to recognize their own patterns of Whiteness or might react defensively when a colleague calls them into race-based conversation. Emotion, in this case, is a clue to possible generative growth. In fact, because huddling in situ demands spontaneity, it affords each participant in the coaching relationship a plethora of data on which to critically reflect. To learn to bring live classroom data into discussions, each of us must examine our assumptions carefully and with a more collective analysis. When we become adept at huddling, we open a space that embraces the tensions that ultimately create positive change.

POWER IN INSTITUTIONAL ROLES

In huddling, we must consider how people's roles, responsibilities, and power might affect the coaching interactions and relationship between the coach and the teacher. Huddling momentarily interrupts the flow and action of the teaching and learning to create a still frame. The person who initiates the huddle, or pauses the action, is exercising power in the moment. If one person is more novice, they may feel uncomfortable initiating the huddle, but as time goes on and the relationship grows, their hesitancy may lessen.

When a coaching relationship also hinges on the coach's duty to complete more-formal evaluations, it can be easy or natural for a teacher to default to the coach as the expert. The teacher might feel as if it is the coach's job to give feedback so that they can grow as a teacher. If the coach considers themselves the expert who holds all the teaching knowledge, and they think the other teacher should only receive feedback, then the coach must do additional work to reposition themselves as a fellow educator, problem-solving *together*. We recommend that you do not provide a list of prompts or questions for huddling in professional development settings, as you might too easily slip into the role of always asking the questions and listening and thus driving the conversation with the teacher. This perspective limits the teacher's ability to reflect critically on their own practice, because they know their coach will tell them what to do and how to improve.

You might imagine how the active decision to pause might be interpreted differently by the educators and learners in the classroom. For example, a teacher might sometimes value or prioritize the learners in the moment over their own decision-making and learning.[10] However, the teacher might also feel the responsibility of responding to their coach, whose role has much power in the institutional school setting.

Let's consider these power dynamics in a few scenarios. These prompts can be a springboard for conversations between an educator and a coach to make space for huddling to confer as part of justice-focused coaching.

How can you make space in the school day for huddling to confer?

- Engage in ongoing and transparent conversations with the coaching community about the hesitation you might feel about supposed interruptions to teaching and learning. You can talk about this tension, and how comfortable each person is with the idea of pausing in the moment. Consider the relative power of everyone in relation to the institution (e.g., school or teacher education programs).

- Discuss the reasons for huddling and the invitations (affirmation, wondering, or disruption) and how those three invitations might be used in relation to the purpose of the huddle. For example, if an administrator is huddling, which invitations will help them understand the teachers' work in the classroom? If a field supervisor is huddling, how might these invitations help them know the learners and the community better?
- Engage in frequent postexperience reflections with one another, asking questions such as, How did that feel, What worked for you, and How might I better support you?
- Practice the language of a huddle in coaching sessions through various scenarios. Play out what might happen when the flow of the classroom gets momentarily paused for reflection. How does each person in the coaching relationship feel during the practice of the huddle?

How can you ensure that your huddling moments are justice-focused?

- Using the observation tool and working with one another, look at the huddling moments that occurred in a classroom event. Huddling, because it is quick, can provide *direct* advice instead of guiding another teacher to develop their own solutions.[11] Consider what you see. What were the purposes and outcomes of each huddle? In what ways are you disrupting expert–novice divides with this coaching tool?
- Consider the focus of the huddles. How are considerations of justice, which are important for the educators, learners, families, and communities, prioritized in the huddles? How can you continue to use huddles to create ripples of change throughout your spheres of influence?

Justice-focused coaching requires that we continually consider these roles and responsibilities. The roles and power dynamics might change throughout the school year, but huddling is based on opening a channel of communication between the coach and the teacher. In using this book together, you might find that power and responsibilities within these roles you hold are becoming clearer because of the sustained conversations you are building together.

HUDDLING TO CONFER: A PRACTICAL GUIDE

What follows is a set of practical suggestions for huddling to confer so you can get started. Recall, however, that context is important—you may need to be flexible to make space for huddling as a coaching tool.

Step 1. Check In, and Conduct Research

The huddle often starts with a lead-in question that attends to the person doing the work. An open-ended invitation like "How's it going?" or "Is this a good time to check in or confer?" combined with eye contact helps you begin the conversation. Drawing on this lead-in, a coach might follow this open-ended question with some research into what is happening in the moment for the teacher: "Is there something I can think through with you?" and then "Can you show me what you're puzzling about or wondering about?" These check-ins and thoughtful analyses might initially feel awkward and one-sided, as the person who is initiating the conference may worry about interrupting the work or the flow of the classroom activities or driving the conversation too strongly. These conversations can also feel rehearsed if the coach uses the same opening each time. However, the language that you use will eventually become more natural and familiar as the coaching partnership develops and as both parties continue to respond to the events of the classroom together.

We should make sure that our purpose for these check-ins and research guides us whenever an opportunity presents itself to implement a huddle. We must think quickly and decide whether the check-in will be to affirm and call out the learners' strengths, to provide a suggestion, or to reteach. In another example of her coaching, Aguilar discusses her relationship with a teacher who has been teaching without student engagement and who values compliance and silence in his classroom. Aguilar asks herself whether she will first address Glasser's teaching or his beliefs about teaching and learning that undergird those beliefs. She writes, "We must address both at the same time."[12] She reflects that both teaching actions or practices and beliefs about teaching, however, must be facilitated through trust and that changes in beliefs will guide changes in behaviors and vice versa. The coach may decide to focus on beliefs more often after an event and to confer around practice while the work continues to unfold in the classroom.

The coach can decide which type of huddling would be best in a teaching event, considering a teacher's practice or their beliefs. Each of the three types of huddling (affirmation, wondering, and disruption) has its own characteristics, but we encourage you to think of the types as fluid. Sometimes a huddling conversation can include wondering and a disruption at the same time. Try not to get bogged down with identifying the perfect or best huddling type, because huddling should be quick and will start to become organic. The beauty of huddling is that it captures a teaching moment and brings to life the thinking behind a of teaching decision.

As a coach, you might be observing the dance of the classroom with a video conferencing platform. If so, the chat can function as the main channel of communication for a huddle between both teachers and learners. Chat can also be used to send private messages that act as a huddle between the teacher and instructional coach, for example.

The quick and private message does not have to interrupt the flow of the class. Rather, the coach can see huddle from the teacher and adjust accordingly. Similarly, text messages or collaborative writing documents like Google Docs can provide a chance to virtually huddle. The benefit of the virtual chat is that it can be saved and used as a reflection document later in the process.

Step 2. Implement the Huddle

Now it is time to initiate a huddling conversation, whether it is an affirmation, something you're wondering about, or a disruption of a belief or a practice from the teacher. Coaches need to think about their specific situation before implementing a huddle. As a coach, are you a co-teacher who is embedded in the life of the classroom? Or do you come into the classroom only once a week? You might also be a coach through a university education program that is working with student teachers. Regardless of your familiarity with the circumstances, the first few huddling conversations might feel uncomfortable because you are new to the setting, and that is okay. You might feel as though you should be in the back of the classroom and passively take notes on the observation. But just as is the case with actively observing, the coach should be with the teacher during the events.

The implementation of a huddling conversation has two aspects: the channel of communication and the resulting action in the class. For example, after deciding on a huddle based on something they're wondering about a practice, the coach could wait for a lull in the class activities. For example, the coach could wait until the learners are working independently or in groups. The coach would then stand side by side with the teacher. As we recommended in step 1, it is helpful to have a way to start the conference without jumping straight into commenting on the other person's teaching practices. The coach might start with a greeting that includes the teacher's name to bring humanity into coaching, which can sometimes be overly focused on constant feedback. The initial language that starts a huddle is like breaking the fourth wall in a play, because it helps both the teacher and the coach detach themselves from the classroom events. Both people can step into the coaching relationship wherein the coach acts as another set of eyes on the classroom events.

In the implementation, the coach can acknowledge and summarize what is going on with both the teacher and the learners in the classroom and what led up to the decision to confer. This acknowledgment recognizes the collective community that also includes the coach. Thinking back to the information gathered from the step 1 conversation, the coach might want to use as inspiration for the huddle the specific practice that the teacher wants to work on.

Because the coach might be the one initiating most of the huddles in the beginning, these sentence starters are helpful for practicing the language of a huddle. As the relationship continues to build on the basis of trust, the teachers also begin to identify moments in their own teaching that they want to highlight with their coach. When teachers initiate a huddle, they begin to break down the vast hierarchical divide between teacher and coach.

Step 3. Keep Track for the Debrief

As we mentioned earlier, huddling captures a teaching moment or decision. But how can we preserve the language around huddling? We have found that the huddling leads to a springboard for discussions in the debriefing time after the lesson. In one single classroom lesson, so many events can take place that it can be difficult for the teacher and coach to remember every detail, let alone the one moment of huddling. For this reason, it is helpful to have a system to quickly record the huddling for both the teacher and the coach.

During her observations of teacher candidates, one of us (Claire) used her observation notes as a place to document the huddling that occurred. Her notes encompassed the three stages of the process: notes from her conversation with the student teacher before the lesson (also known as the preconference), a transcript of the lesson, and notes from her conversation with the teacher after the lesson (also known as the postconference). During the lesson, Claire used a T-chart; the left side was a transcript of the lesson events, and the right side included her thoughts and reflections.

On the left-hand side, Claire recorded her huddling, including *who* initiated it, because she wanted to track this aspect of the huddling over time. The coach might realize that they are the ones mostly initiating the huddle. This kind of tracking could be an opportunity for the coach to critically examine power dynamics and, perhaps in the future, to empower the teacher to actively reflect on, and ask questions about, their teaching practices in the middle of a lesson. Claire also noted *how* the huddling took place in the classroom. Does it always occur in the back of the classroom? Does it occur at a table with learners? Does the huddle happen in a virtual chat setting? Again, tracking this information can help coaches see how the huddling evolved. It also helps coaches get curious about their own practices and tendencies with huddling. When we document our huddles, we save a snapshot of a moment within the lesson. As the coach, we have the freedom to observe and remember aspects of the lesson that the teacher might be too close to, or too busy with, to make the same observations.

Typically, quality is more important than quantity in terms of the number of huddles used in any teaching event. Shoot for one or two meaningful huddles. As the huddle becomes a part of your ways of collaborating in the classroom, this number may increase.

Step 4. Debrief

In our own research, we find the debrief of an observation to be the most fruitful space of the coaching that focuses on teacher learning. Most of our own research and that of others focuses on the postconference portion of an observation cycle (see chapter 5). To discuss debriefing in a huddle, we will adapt our ideas about debriefing in a coaching cycle. Huddling is different from the longer coaching cycle because of the pause in action that a huddle requires. In our debriefing conversation with teachers, we want to carve out some space to unpack the moment or event that inspired the huddle. Table 4.1 is a guide to the debriefing.

You will inevitably have to choose a focus before your debriefing, as you do not want this postconference to last a long time. You have important planning and next steps to consider as part of your coaching! The first choice is how to open the conversation. Here we might elicit some sensory memories, such as what an event sounded like or

TABLE 4.1 *Huddling to confer: A debriefing guide*

Open the conversation	• What was happening in the moment when we decided to huddle? • What else do you remember about that moment?
Reflect on the huddle	• Was the huddle to affirm, wonder about, or disrupt something? What happened because one of us made that choice in the moment? What might have happened if we had chosen a different pathway into this conference? • What are we noticing, over time, about our choices in huddling? Are particular kinds of discussions initiated more often than others? What might account for these patterns?
Generate new knowledge about teaching	• What were the benefits of the teaching move you made for justice or equity in the classroom? What storyline or storylines did this disrupt? • How can we continue to move forward with this teaching move, over time? • How can we continue, tomorrow and every day, to repeat in the classroom the justice-focused action you just described?
Generalize to broader issues of justice	• At that moment, what did we believe about students and learning? • What interrupted or disrupted that belief, and what new beliefs are we developing? • How might we generalize this new belief to other beliefs that might be holding us back from changing our practice?

looked like in that moment. Perhaps a surprising action or surge in volume in the classroom spurred the huddle, or it might have been a quiet, calm moment that provided the co-teachers some time to pause and observe the action. The next step is to reflect on the huddle itself. Finally, we want to make sense of the teaching event in a way that will, like the postconference step described in a coaching cycle, lead to new actions or a better understanding of the complex and personal act of teaching. For example, we might want to make an immediate plan for the teacher's next lesson using what we learned in our debriefing. A person with more coaching expertise might provide an additional nudge for the teacher in these moments, suggesting a generalization that can be made from the event.

Another focus in debriefing can be to connect practice with belief. We find these debriefing experiences to be rich opportunities for justice-focused coaching. It is easy to stop before this point and stay on the surface of the teaching that unfolded during the lesson. But by shifting your attention to a justice-oriented lens, you can see what might be underneath the interactions and dynamics in the classroom. The reasons we often miss this step are attributed to time— we don't have time to take this extra step to puzzle about what we don't yet know.

Unfortunately, discussions of equity are even more elusive in coaching, supposedly because of a lack of time, resources, or opportunities. But we have found that, rather, many people choose not to prioritize these discussions. For us White teachers and teacher educators, these conversations are often painful because we must come to terms with how past and current practices have harmed learners. And for all educators, especially teachers of Color who work closely with White people, these conversations can also be painful. In our teacher education program, field supervisors of Color have shared their experiences of being the only teacher educators to address racism and Whiteness with teacher candidates, and the resistance that they encounter. We must make conscious choices to take these extra steps in a debriefing conversation to disrupt what has for too long been ignored.

The following case study documents Claire's experiences with huddling to confer in an online coaching experience. This example illustrates the step-by-step process Claire used as a field supervisor working with interns she had not yet met (virtually or in person) in early summer of 2020, just as education went remote in response to the global pandemic. We will highlight how huddling to confer helped Claire and others build relationships toward justice-focused teaching in this new, remote community of teachers and teacher educators.

CLAIRE'S STORY

During the summer of 2020, Claire was coaching during a global pandemic that necessitated all teaching, learning, and consequently her coaching to happen remotely. She was at a bit of a loss, as the former coaching cycles she had used with interns in face-to-face settings seemed to be out of reach in this new remote environment. As an instructional coach and a graduate student in an urban teacher education program, she was coaching teachers in a summer middle-school youth program, for the first time in a virtual setting. The teachers were new to the profession and unfamiliar with teaching in virtual spaces. When she brought her experiences back to our research meetings and we reflected on small adjustments she might make to refine her practices as a coach, we brought up the use of huddling to confer. In one meeting, a team member remarked, "It sounds like you need a coaching tool like the huddle we've used in early internship classrooms, but a virtual huddle." The idea took off and allowed a channel of communication between Claire and the teachers.

Claire noticed two problems of practice in this virtual setting (1) the teachers were struggling to connect with their learners as most of the students chose to have their cameras and microphones off, and (2) the teachers had difficulty forming an intentional and united classroom community without the normal face to face interactions.

Step 1. Check In, and Conduct Research

Claire met with the group of teachers she was coaching and suggested that they try huddling to coach in the virtual classroom. Together, the teachers connected the idea of huddling with their pedagogy. They had learned to confer with students in their literacy methods coursework, and they saw the connections. We have seen this before—when we focus on coaching collaboratively with our colleagues, we often find connections between the ways we can disrupt expert–novice binaries and focus on justice in our coaching and our own pedagogy. Even though Claire was the coach, she was honest with the teachers, explaining that she had never taught in a virtual setting before and was therefore not an expert in this new way of teaching and learning. Rather, this virtual huddling was an opportunity for them to learn together how to create new pathways for coaching.

Claire took some time to work on her own groundwork for opening this conversation with the preservice teachers. Before meeting with them, she wrote notes about the affordances and constraints of the virtual classroom and what she wanted to focus on in her coaching. She found she needed more information, so after their first week of online teaching, Claire met with these eight preservice teachers. She asked, "How does it feel to teach in this new virtual setting?"

The teachers expressed a wide range of emotions. Some felt some success and others felt discouraged. But all their energies seemed to be devoted to finding ways to connect with learners—who had their cameras off—evidence of the technological barriers of teaching remotely. Claire understood and appreciated their concerns because she knew how important it was for learners to feel heard and seen in class. As a collective, Claire and the preservice teachers brainstormed ways to encourage learners to participate during class and decided to use the private chat function on Zoom to message learners directly. The hope was that this tactic could open a channel of dialogue between the teachers and their learners, as well as a focus point for Claire during her observations and huddles.

Step 2. Implement the Huddle

One afternoon, technology became a barrier to instruction. As a coach, Claire was observing Jacky teach a lesson to a group of six middle school learners. Jacky was teaching in a Zoom classroom where all the learners had turned off their cameras and their microphones. Jacky was trying to explain to the learners how to rename themselves on Zoom so that she could positively interact with individual learners she could not see. Since this was the beginning of using Zoom for learning purposes, the students struggled to find the correct button to change their name. Claire observed Jacky start to grow frustrated as the teacher explained, several times, how to change a screen name on Zoom. It was not even clear if the students understood her directions, since no one was asking for clarification aloud or even in the virtual chat area on the screen. As Claire was observing the lesson, she noticed that one student, Simon, understood Jacky's directions and had successfully changed his screen name. Perhaps thinking back to the earlier conversation with the teachers about the power of the chat function on Zoom, Claire privately messaged Jacky: "Maybe Simon could explain to the learners how he renamed himself?"

Seeing the message, Jacky's face lit up as she asked Simon if he could teach the class how he figured out the process of renaming himself. Eager to help his classmates, Simon unmuted his microphone and talked through the directions in his own way. Across the screen, the names of the learners slowly changed. Somehow sensing the power of conferring or intuitively seeing the power of the community to solve problems together, another student, Josh, sent a message to his classmates in the chat offering that he could help his classmates if they were still confused. This was the first time a student had participated, and it was such a powerful moment for Clair and Jacky to see ripple effects.

Step 3. Keep Track for the Debrief

Claire was using the template shown in 4.1 for her observations, and she continued to take notes as Jacky and Simon's interaction unfolded. Figure 4.3 shows the first part of the template, what was happening before the huddle. In the left-hand column of the figure, you can see the observations that Claire jotted as she listened. Note that these were not extensive or difficult to collect, but they were noteworthy to Claire because of the justice focus identified by the preservice teachers, who were concerned with connecting to students. In the right-hand column, Claire connected her observation to a reflection to share later with Jacky.

After seeing the confusion, Claire decided to huddle with Jacky to *wonder* about a possible idea (see figure 4.4). In reflection, this choice of a huddling invitation reflected the teachers' entry into the idea of student engagement in the virtual classroom. The idea that a coach wonders about is not something they command or expects adherence to. Instead, the wondering is a suggestion, authentically posed to try something out as a member of this professional community, and Claire went for it. She asked Jacky if Simon might be in the po-

FIGURE 4.3 *Applied observation tool: Before huddling to confer*

Observation date: 07/21/2021	Who is present, and what are their roles? *Claire (CC): instructional coach* *Jacky (JM): teacher* *Middle school students*

Mode of observation (circle one):   **In Person**   (**Live video**)

Context (circle one):   **Co-teaching**   (**Transparent observer**)   **Outside observer**

Observational data	Reflections
10:40 a.m. JM: *Today is all about practicing for your presentations. We want you to rename yourself to include your group number. So please go ahead and do that right now. I see that Simon has done it.* JM: *If you look at my name, you can see that I already changed it.* Student: *Do I have to sign out of Zoom to do that?*	*There seemed to be a lot of confusion here, so I am glad that you took the time to go over this concept. Especially since they might be nervous about their presentations tomorrow.*

sition to take on a role as explainer or trainer, encouraging others to change their screen names so they could be known. After the invitation, Claire continued to take notes to capture the action that ensued.

Again writing in the right-hand column, Claire recorded her reflections on the huddle. She first recognized how the huddle served to encourage wondering but also disrupted a possible inequity in the classroom. Claire intentionally wanted Simon to be positioned as a powerful teacher in the classroom, thus disrupting what could have

FIGURE 4.4 *Applied observation tool: During huddling to confer*

Observation date: 07/21/2021	Who is present, and what are their roles? *Claire (CC): instructional coach* *Jacky (JM): teacher* *Middle school students*

Mode of observation (circle one): **In Person** (**Live video**)

Context (circle one): **Co-teaching** (**Transparent observer**) **Outside observer**

Observational data	Reflections
During huddle CC to JM (private message in the chat): *I am wondering if Simon could explain to the other students how he changed his screen name. He could maybe offer the student perspective.* JM: *Simon, I am wondering if you could maybe show us how you changed your screen name to the class. Maybe you could explain it in a way that's easier so that other students could understand?* Simon [unmutes]: *I do have a Chromebook. I went to Participants, and then right next to my name, I saw a circle with two arrows, and it shows two options Mute or Rename.* JM: *Great, thank you!* Josh [in the chat]: *I can also help.* [The names start to change on the screen.]	*This huddle acted both to disrupt a teaching practice and to allow us to wonder about an alternative. I offered a suggestion, something that could be implemented but that was not required of Jacky. In addition, I wanted to position the student as the expert and as someone capable of always helping his peers.* *Great adjustment here, being able to have Simon be the expert! Then notice how Josh also wanted to help his classmates. Great opportunity for building a community that supports each other.*

quickly escalated into a situation where students would push back or continue to be silent because of a technological barrier.

Step 4. Debrief

The result of the huddle was positive. Simon was the first student to unmute himself and share out loud, inspiring the other learners to be brave as well.

Claire's huddle to confer with Jacky was a quick, momentary move of the coach to stop the action, name the problem of practice, and provide a window into her thinking as a coach. It was not that Jacky could not solve this problem herself, but rather, the new teacher was responsible for many actions at that moment, all in a new virtual setting. Claire, as an observer, had more mental room to analyze what was happening. The conference solved a problem but also created a shared experience that Claire and Jacky could later reflect on and share with the larger group of teachers who were learning to teach on Zoom.

During a major shift in the context of teaching, educators will often need to adapt, as Claire did, to the changing situation. Claire was able to use huddling flexibly across the virtual classrooms to connect with the teachers, to provide an affirming, wondering, or disruptive huddle, to support the teaching flow.

Roles, Responsibilities, and Power in This Story

Claire held a position as a field supervisor, which in this setting meant she was both a member of a critical professional community and someone in a position to evaluate the learning and growth of the eight preservice teachers. Early in this experience, she prioritized her role as a member of the professional community to collaboratively problem-solve with the teachers. Fortunately, this new exclusively virtual context was full of puzzles and possibilities and allowed Claire to take on a role as co-inquirer through the huddles. She still had power in this situation. Jacky probably felt compelled to take up the suggestion in that moment, as her field supervisor had directed, especially with the knowledge that Claire would eventually be providing a more formal evaluation as part of the teacher education requirements. These power dynamics are important for you to identify and to discuss in a debriefing conference. You may want to consider how and when, as a coach or co-teacher, you may have similar opportunities in the moment to build strategic, learner-centered practices with others and to transparently engage in discussions about roles, power, and responsibilities.

CONCLUSION

Huddling to confer builds on and complements actively observing practice together as a justice-focused coaching tool. For coaches, huddling is more flexible than a traditional observation cycle and is an appropriate choice when they are starting a coaching relationship. It is an opportunity to pause the dance of the classroom to observe practice together, to develop and revise teaching practices that are more just for learners.

You might want to revisit chapter 3 to reexamine the importance of critical self-reflection, vulnerability, humility, and facilitation in all the coaching tools that we introduce in this book. If you can continue to reflect on the benefits and challenges of these coaching tools, you will grow as a coach. As you move back into your coaching work, pay attention to how you select a huddle—what feels more comfortable and when it feels harder to disrupt inequities in the classroom during huddles. You may be tempted to settle into a comfortable rhythm, but we encourage you, like Claire, to take an inquiry perspective when huddling and to continue to grow as a justice-focused educator.

—— CHAPTER 5 ——

JUSTICE-FOCUSED COACHING CYCLES

The coaching cycle, a formal structure we build on in this chapter, is recognizable across different teacher learning settings and builds from these two previously discussed tools: actively observing practice together and huddling to confer. Coaching cycles are common in initial teacher certification, specialist certification, and in-service programs for teacher development and evaluation. Professional learning communities also use coaching cycles for learning and professional growth. As a reader of this book, you probably have used coaching cycles in more than one of these contexts.

The structure of a formal coaching cycle has been studied by many researchers and professional development experts. In your teaching or coaching, you may have encountered foundational scholarship such as Jim Knight's instructional coaching and Arthur Costa and Robert Garmston's cognitive coaching.[1] Many school districts and programs have begun implementing professional learning for mentors, preparing teacher leaders and coaches to use cycles more effectively. Programs such as cognitive coaching, instructional coaching, and transformational coaching are often adopted by a program, school, or district seeking to bolster coaching through professional development.[2] Typically, these forms of professional development follow the same perspectives that are embedded in the coaching cycle and are taught with a directive model that includes evaluations for fidelity and impact on learners.

In our research with Coaching with CARE, we worked with mentors of preservice teachers first to better understand the model of cognitive coaching and then to begin innovating with teachers, drawing on critical pedagogical frameworks.[3] The justice-focused coaching cycle departs from other models in that professional learning opportunities for coaches begin with honoring their histories and experiences with coaching and building practices together within communities. Further, these coaching cycles prioritize issues of equity and justice in the classroom with the goal of disrupting dominant ways of knowing.

PAUSE AND REFLECT

How might your local community benefit from a coaching cycle focused on justice? What conflicts might you prepare for when introducing coaching cycles focused on justice?

We begin this chapter with some background on the justice-focused coaching cycle and some practical templates for working with this tool. In this chapter's case study, one of us (Heather) worked with a preservice teacher, Madelyn, and Madelyn's cooperating teacher, Lori. As the triad engaged in multiple cycles of teaching, observing, and coaching, they focused on equitable practices in their kindergarten classroom. We will share how the team's situation and coaching actions helped facilitate coaching cycles toward justice. We will also show how Heather used these templates.

BACKGROUND: WHAT IS A JUSTICE-FOCUSED COACHING CYCLE?

Coaching cycles are iterative practices of conversation, observation, and action that expand on actively observing practice together. Figure 5.1, a template for a justice-focused coaching cycle, resembles

FIGURE 5.1 *Template observation tool: Justice-focused coaching cycle*

Observation date: ___ / ___ / ___	Who is present, and what are their roles?

Mode of observation (circle one):   **In Person   Live Video**

Context (circle one):   **Co-teaching   Transparent observer   Outside observer**

Preconference discussion
- What do we know about this community's needs and desires?
- What have we agreed to focus on today?

Observational data	**Reflections**
Which classroom observations are related to the community **situation** and preconference goals?	What might you affirm, wonder about, or disrupt? What new questions do you have? Be specific.
Explicitly record what you see and hear happening in the classroom. Time and action will move quickly! Having a specific focus will guide your data collection. Consider interactional data such as direct dialogue, body language, and physical arrangement of tools and space.	

Reflection discussion
- Return to your shared definitions and vision of equity and justice.
- What actions were captured in your notes? What was the impact on the learners?
- In light of your discussion, what might be the focus of a future observation?

Postconference discussion
- What have you been thinking about since you taught the lesson?
- (Specific planned questions based on observational data.)

the template for actively observing practice together. However, in this template, there is an increased focus on the coaching that occurs before and after an observation. During those times, conversations about practice are extended in some increasingly formal structures and sharpen the focus on issues of justice in the classroom.

We use the metaphor of a cycle to describe this coaching tool because, while there is a linear process to follow between a preconference, an observation, and a postconference (often called a POP cycle), there is also an iterative, circular quality to this process. The postconference is likely to reveal new learning and questions that can lead into the next preconference and observation. Therefore, each part of the cycle depends on (and informs) the next part of the cycle. Some models like Coaching with CARE and cognitive coaching add an additional dimension of planning to the POP cycle. These models add a way for the learnings from the coaching cycle to be extended into planning for subsequent teaching. As we explore some big ideas, we will also share a few additional tools for focusing your discussions in coaching cycles.

The Multiple Orientations of Justice-Focused Coaching Cycles

Like many other aspects of education, coaching cycles benefit from a well-rounded approach composed of many perspectives. Let's look at the four important orientations that contribute to our work with justice-focused coaching cycles.

A HUMANISTIC ORIENTATION. We have suggested that coaches must build relationships that are based on curiosity and must continuously seek to understand how teachers define their goals for the learners and the classroom community. A humanistic approach focuses and builds on the personhood of those being coached; it values their thoughts and feelings. Starting from a humanistic perspective, a cycle starts with and builds from a core question: What have you been thinking about since the teaching event? Throughout the cycles, and especially during preconferences, coaches ask clarifying questions about their teachers' visions, so that meaning can be defined first by the teacher. By prioritizing a teacher's goals, a coach can then focus on the alignment of beliefs and practice. A humanistic approach is crucial to justice-focused coaching because it asks the coach to think about the expertise and experience of the person being coached in settings that may lean toward an evaluative purpose for coaching.

Figure 5.2 shows a coaching cycle in which the coach is drawing from a humanistic perspective. You'll notice the focus is appreciative, building on the idea of a learning conference we drew on in huddling. The questions highlight the teachers' goals for their teaching and their experience of the teaching event that is the focus of observation.

You might be wondering, What if a teacher's identity and goals are not yet focused on justice or critical consciousness? What happens

FIGURE 5.2 *Humanistic orientation of a justice-focused coaching cycle*

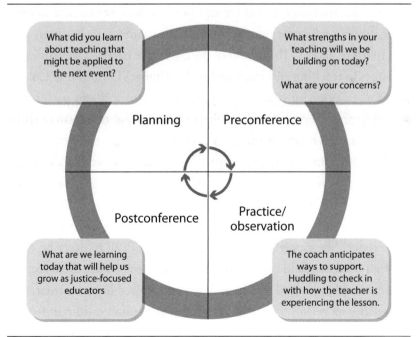

What did you learn about teaching that might be applied to the next event?

What strengths in your teaching will we be building on today?

What are your concerns?

Planning

Preconference

Postconference

Practice/
observation

What are we learning today that will help us grow as justice-focused educators

The coach anticipates ways to support. Huddling to check in with how the teacher is experiencing the lesson.

when a teacher does not organically bring up justice-oriented goals for teaching in the classroom or is not yet connecting justice to their identities and goals? Many injustices in the classroom can fester when we do not address them or when we wait for others to notice them. We encourage you to reflect on the additional coaching tools in this book as a resource in navigating teachers' (and coaches') different locations along the justice-focused continuum of teaching.

BEHAVIORAL AND COGNITIVE ORIENTATIONS.   Justice-focused coaching cycles also draw from behavioral and cognitive orientations. These perspectives prime a coach to think about change as reflected in both the teacher's behavior and their decision-making. A behavioral orientation, like the humanistic perspective, focuses on what is happening in the classroom; a coach might closely document the language and interactions in the classroom (see figure 5.3). Conversations focus on changes made and the impact of those changes on the learner.

Besides attending to beliefs and perspectives, we must also consider how an educator's decisions reflect a connection between perspective and action. This is where the cognitive perspective comes in. Changes in teaching and learning involve changes in thinking. Coaching is not a one-and-done activity; it focuses on shifts in patterns of knowing and doing over time. Figure 5.4 highlights the small shifts in how coaches might approach a cycle from a cognitive perspective.

By definition, an iterative process is done again and again, arguably to improve the process. One of our colleagues, Alycia Maurer, at Our Lady of the Lake University, brainstormed with us about the ways a cycle could lead to an additional observation and subsequent conference. She cleverly used the acronym POPOP to describe what she had tried as a field supervisor. After the initial postconference, the student teacher invited Alycia back to see a revised lesson format, and the field supervisor conducted an additional observation and post-conference based on the action plan from the first postconference.

FIGURE 5.3 *Behavioral orientation of justice-focused coaching cycle*

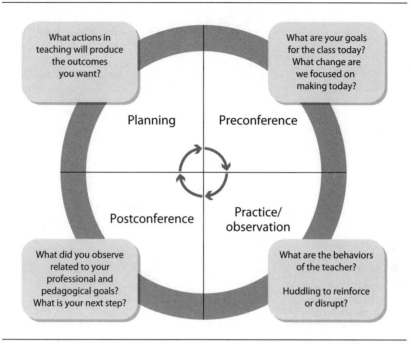

While time is not always a resource that a coach has, we encourage coaches to take a step back to examine the observations they may be required to complete with teachers. Look closely for ways to bring continuity to discussions around equity and justice in the classroom. In this way, you are constantly building on the knowledge of tensions, injustices, and oppressive practices that are relevant to the specific teaching situation.

We have often seen cycles used in schools for accountability or professional development, but typically there are only one or two opportunities for a coach or an administrator to engage in a cycle with an educator. Jennifer Jacobs, Kristine Hogarty, and Rebecca West Burns looked across a large number of elementary teacher education programs. They found that few respondents to their survey had

FIGURE 5.4 *Cognitive orientation of justice-focused coaching cycle*

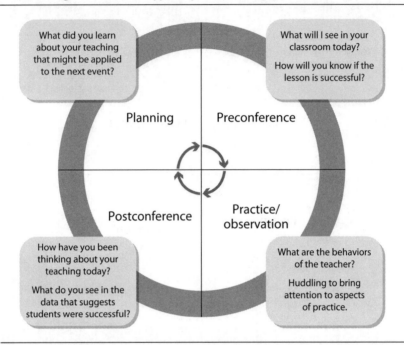

designed their programs so that field supervisors could stay with pre-service teachers over multiple semesters.[4] This lack of continuity may influence a coach's ability to form the relationships necessary to engage in justice-focused coaching cycles. The repetitive nature of justice-focused cycles within the life of teacher–coach relationship allows the dyad to intentionally make space for issues of justice in the classroom.

CRITICAL ORIENTATION. Finally, critical perspectives are important in a justice-focused coaching cycle because they orient a coach and an educator to locate dominant perspectives that may exclude other perspectives, namely, those of learners, their families, and colleagues. To investigate how racism, ableism, sexism, and monolingualism show up in the classroom, all parties must grow and work together. In our research, we have found that conversations slowly solidify people's connections, forming a strong foundation as coaching relationships and justice-focused practices grow. To participate in a cycle from a critical orientation, we must understand how issues of justice are important across many spheres of influence. Although critically focused coaching cycles are the least common in the literature, they hold great promise for disrupting hierarchies of power and orienting teacher learning toward equity and justice. For example, Charlotte Land has documented the ways that retrospective video analysis and responsive critical discourse analysis serve as coaching tools to help keep coaching cycle conversations focused on critical conversations close to the language and activity in the classroom.[5] Figure 5.5 is an example of language in a critically focused coaching cycle.

FIGURE 5.5 *Critical orientation of justice-focused coaching cycle*

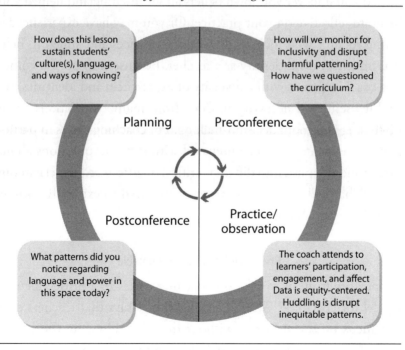

How does this lesson sustain students' culture(s), language, and ways of knowing?

How will we monitor for inclusivity and disrupt harmful patterning? How have we questioned the curriculum?

Planning

Preconference

Postconference

Practice/observation

What patterns did you notice regarding language and power in this space today?

The coach attends to learners' participation, engagement, and affect Data is equity-centered. Huddling is disrupt inequitable patterns.

PAUSE AND REFLECT

Take a moment to reflect on what we've shared so far about these four orientations within the coaching cycle: behavioral, cognitive, humanistic, and critical. Prior to this moment, what approaches have you drawn from when engaging in coaching? What evidence do you have of these orientations in your practice? What has each perspective contributed toward teacher learning and student experience?

These figures are starting places. In them, we emphasize several reasons why we need to include multiple orientations in coaching. First, the teachers who are participating in coaching cycles are not blank slates. Perhaps as a novice teacher, you were coached by someone who had great influence on you, and they were oriented from a cognitive perspective. You can recall their patient questions that helped you uncover your own beliefs about teaching and helped you be more reflective on your practice. Or you may have experienced a caring mentor who focused on your experiences and aimed to help you find your own identity as a teacher. Because each person comes to a coaching event with a diversity of experiences and identities, we find it useful and necessary to draw from many orientations when discussing classroom decision-making. For coaching cycles in particular, participants can come prepared with different questions about justice and can push into different critical questions around classroom data. What will not vary, however, is the need to explicitly address injustices and who they harm—this is key.

Prioritizing Justice in the Cycle

What does it mean to take on coaching cycles in a justice-focused model for coaching? Gloria Ladson-Billings says that teachers cannot focus on social justice without directly addressing the urgent issues learners and their communities continuously endure in an unjust society characterized by White supremacy, exclusion, and racial violence.[6] But the term *dominant perspectives* is too neutral. Dominant perspectives not only dominate systems like education but also push out alternative and powerful ways of knowing and being in the world. A coaching cycle can become the space where coaches and teachers openly discuss such exclusion as it pertains to the learners in the classroom. This may mean calling out racism, sexism, ableism, and other forms of exclusion and violence when they are happening in the classroom. A coaching cycle can also be a place to scrutinize other classroom and societal injustices like heteronormative language practices, such as using binary language to refer to students as boys and girls, or ladies and gentlemen. Through a coaching cycle, we can work on changes to a classroom environment and reflect a restorative approach to education, privileging belonging over exclusion for the learners who already experience exclusion because of their ethnicity, race, gender, language, or other identities.[7] The examples are expansive, but again, communities will set their priorities according to a shared and inclusive understanding of injustice and justice.

As we will discuss in more detail later, coaches do not always feel equipped to put justice at the center of their coaching. Coaches we have worked with have often begun a coaching cycle with a pedagogical framework, such as Django Paris and H. Samy Alim's culturally sustaining pedagogy.[8] Such a pedagogy depends on the teachers' ability to examine their own histories and identities in relation to the practices they are seeking to build. And as we've noted throughout this book, this critical self-reflection is an ongoing process. Knowing oneself, as Sealey-Ruiz suggests, in her previously discussed archaeology of self framework demands deep reflective study of how we position others and are positioned *by* others in various spaces according to our racial, gender, and other identities.[9] So, assuming that this self-examination work is ongoing in the community, a coaching cycle might begin with a curricular decision, which allows learners to draw on their broad range or repertoire of languages and cultural knowledge. With a pedagogical framework, the coach and teacher can work together to make sure the teaching practices reflects their beliefs. It also creates opportunities for coaches and teachers to share professional resources to layer into the preconference, observation, postconference, and planning sessions. You might imagine how starting with a concrete change to the curriculum or instruction in a coaching cycle might be a strong starting point.

Justice is not about making singular curricular changes but instead is about the pursuit of more equitable systems across spheres of influence. To pursue justice in coaching, you may need your cycles to consider racial literacies, expanding the range of practices that disrupt racist systems. For example, you might ask questions about how race affects a classroom interaction or the learners in the classroom. Sealey-Ruiz suggests that interrupting racism requires a deep awareness of how race has historically operated within systems and still does today and a willingness to name racism when it occurs. As a tool for building new, generative teaching approaches that are more racially just, coaching can explore beliefs about, and histories of, participation in schooling, and how race is operating. We encourage you to consider how you're centering justice in each coaching cycle, drawing from your growing understandings of justice across spheres of influence in your community.

Paying Attention to Language

Language is an important component of justice. Coaches and teachers use language to reflect together and build new understandings about teaching. In a justice-focused coaching cycle, the coach may be responsible for continuing to build this shared orientation. During the observation portion of the cycle, a coach can collect data on themes such as teacher language (is it asset-based or deficit-based?), student language (can the students use their home languages during lessons?), or nonverbal cues (what is the teacher's or students' body language communicating?). The data then becomes a tangible tool for the coach and teacher to engage in justice-focused discussions during the postconference. Additionally, the data from observations can be combined with the critical questions from the debriefing part of actively observing practice together.

Language in coaching becomes self-extending for teachers. One teacher who participated in a justice-focused coaching cycle with her mentor told us, "I actually have a game plan. It's like a toolbox for what I can do when I'm in my own classroom. . . . I have my own experiences now. It's exciting! The language that I am using now, I feel like this will make me be the teacher that I want to be in my head. This is how I'm going to get there; this is what I want. With this, I can impact someone, but they can impact me too." The teacher is reflecting on how her decisions align with her vision as teacher.

POWER IN INSTITUTIONAL ROLES

In previous chapters, we have identified how systems of power dictate the roles and responsibilities of coaches and teachers. While we may not always be able to completely change these systems, our hope in bringing awareness to these issues in coaching is that it will help us to imagine the possibilities. Within the coaching cycle, coaches often have specific roles and responsibilities from the institutions that employ them. For example, institutional roles may come with protocols or practices of coaching that do not, at first glance, lend themselves to conversations around equity and justice in the classroom. Another hurdle may be finding ways to incorporate and honor the voices and needs of the community within a coaching cycle. For example, a coach's predetermined responsibilities may require them to focus on pedagogical content knowledge removed from the cultural context of the learners and their communities.

We offer the following "how can you?" scenarios to help you puzzle through the roles, responsibilities, and power dynamics that might arise in a coaching cycle. Specifically, these scenarios stem from our ultimate goal of justice-focused coaching.

How can you, as a coach and an educator, focus on issues of equity and justice during a coaching cycle while meeting the demands of state-sanctioned evaluations?

- As a coach tied to the evaluations, know the content of the evaluations and the coach's responsibilities. Look for overlap between the required content from state-sanctioned evaluations and justice-focused issues that are relevant to the teacher's classroom context. Often, any connections between state requirements and justice goals, as well as building blocks in one or the other, can help us streamline our focus and conversations, rather than seeing these two as separate burdens.
- Bring the evaluation protocols or guidelines with you to the coaching cycles as a conversation piece with your teachers, colleagues, and teachers. Look together to find the overlap.

How can you, as a coach and an educator, honor the needs of the community within your justice-focused coaching cycles?

- In chapter 3, we discussed how coaches may be seen as outsiders to the school and classroom community. This perception of coaches is a very real and relevant concern. It may not always be appropriate to change your status from outsider to insider. If this is the case, we suggest looking in your spheres of influence to find teachers who are more knowledgeable about the community's needs. Brainstorm together how issues of justice might find a place in the next coaching cycle.

- Be prepared. Do whatever research is possible about the community's needs before you begin your coaching cycles. Find ways to learn about the learners in this space. Work with other teachers to understand the conflicts in this community before making assumptions about what you think is best.

Teachers will continue to grapple with the responsibilities of a coach and the important power dynamics in a coaching cycle, especially as educators turn their focus toward justice in these settings. We hope that by recognizing these very real issues, we can begin to see them as possibilities for change rather than excuses for not doing the work.

JUSTICE-FOCUSED COACHING CYCLES: A PRACTICAL GUIDE

Now that we have taken this deep dive into orientations within coaching cycles and what it means to focus on justice, we return to our practical guide for conducting a coaching cycle. Here, we will discuss the preconference, observation, postconference, and planning conference in more detail.

Step 1. The Preconference

The preconference is typically a short meeting before the teaching begins. We think of it as the invitation to the observation. Orienting questions might sound like "What change are we focused on making today?" (see figure 5.1) or "What strengths in your teaching will we be focusing on today?" (see figure 5.3).

> **PAUSE AND REFLECT**
>
> You may now be wondering how to decide where to begin. What is one of your core beliefs about coaching? Think about this core belief, and revisit figures 5.1 through 5.4. Which question in the preconference speaks to this core belief about coaching?

If you answered that coaching should be focused on the teacher's needs and desires, you may be drawn to the humanistic orientation. If you believe that coaching should be grounded in horizontal expertise—or honoring the knowledge of both teachers in the room—you might be drawn into another choice, such as the cognitive orientation. In the preconference, you will want to establish why you are doing the observation and how you will interact during it. You will also want to establish in the preconference what practices or outcomes you have identified with the person you're coaching, and your community, in your analysis of inequities or injustices. The preconference might also extend to community in other ways, propelling you to ask, "What larger issues, local events, or national news might affect the community and have an impact on this observation and coaching cycle?"

The preconference also includes a decision about how two or more people will engage with one another and with learners during the observation, for example, when coach and learners are actively observing practice together. This is where the first aspect of social justice-focused coaching becomes relevant: how can you disrupt the expert–novice divide in terms of roles in the teaching observation? Typically, we must scrutinize the roles, responsibilities, and power of the people involved, and even if the purpose is compliance, those involved can expand and clarify the purpose of the observation. Or perhaps the purpose of this observation is not for compliance or documentation but is to learn about a particular classroom practice or about a student or learners in the classroom. For example, one third-grade teacher we work with found several learners who were continuously scoring low on benchmark assessments in reading comprehension, and the learners were Black children who she suspected had not been provided with engaging and relevant materials in previous grades. The teacher wanted to engage in coaching cycles to better support learners with culturally relevant materials. She asked her observer to co-observe what her learners were doing during independent reading time—how they were reading the culturally responsive texts—to learn more about their reading practices. In the postconference, she worked with her observer to reflect on and then design some additional actions that might support the learners.

Once roles and expectations are established, then it's time to create a plan for data collection. In the example above, the observer was watching the learners while the other held responsibility for overseeing other activities in the classroom. If each person is working with a small group of learners, they might jot down some brief notes or use a smartphone to capture the conversation to return to later. In the preconference, the teachers might decide what to focus on in collecting notes because it is very difficult to capture everything. Planning your roles together during the preconference can help focus everyone's attention on what all of you are hoping to capture as you take notes.

One virtual modification that several field supervisors in our program made for the preconference involved collaborative writing instead of a face-to-face preconference on Zoom. This modification made sense because many of our preservice teachers and field supervisors had identified their fatigue with Zoom, as they were also teaching and observing on Zoom during the school day because of limited access to the classroom during Covid-19 and social distancing. Virtual modifications are important to keep in mind when there are constraints on the context of coaching in your setting.

Step 2. The Observation

As an extension of the preconference, the observation is focused and purposeful. You might want to revisit chapter 3 to think about your decision-making during this part of the cycle. Again, your orientation to teacher learning will guide you in what you collect. One special education field supervisor we work with closely was interested in supporting preservice teachers who were learning to interact equitably with learners with special needs in an inclusive classroom. The purpose was to understand how learners who received individualized education accommodations were participating in activities such as class discussions and given opportunities to share their strengths in the lesson. The field supervisor used a data collection chart where she collected data about the teacher's and learners' turn-taking—who spoke, for how long, and whether they spoke by invitation or without it—to understand how learners were engaging with the lesson and how the teacher supported those learners. Observation recording tools like this can be part of coaching frameworks such as Jim Knight's impact cycle and can be useful and convenient ways to collect data.[10]

Other observers we know have focused on collecting as much of the learners' talk as possible to help the teacher reflect on the conversations when questions were centered on equity. This attention to power dynamics within classroom discourse is a common approach across critical orientations. For example, a cooperating teacher we worked with was investigating fifth-grade girls' participation in science discussions. She tracked how they participated and how they physically engaged and disengaged during the discussions. Collecting learner data during an observation is a powerful tool. In addition to spoken words, learner data can include other communication modes—body language, drawings, writings. There are many options when it comes to collecting data, but the observations should be tied to the preconference and the justice-focused purpose of the observation.

Finally, there will be times when the observer feels called to enter the action. Sometimes you might want to step in because you believe that you can be of help or you are drawn to huddle. You might notice a learner who needs a bit of support. Or, if you are co-teaching, you may be intentionally working with a learner or group of learners so that later, each teacher can bring their observations and reflections to the postconference. Finding moments during your interactions or after teaching to jot down your notes is essential for documentation. As you find these moments, make sure to emphasize the learners' voices that you heard and interacted with during the observation. Although you can help teachers understand your suggestions by modeling teaching moves in the moment, your documentation of observations focused on what the learners were thinking, saying, and doing will help teachers gain insight into their learners and will help you recenter issues of justice in your coaching cycles.

Like Leighton et al., we have also found that virtual video platforms such as Zoom, Microsoft Teams, and FaceTime are helpful digital tools in the observation.[11] During preconferences and postconferences, these platforms allow coaches to intentionally engage teachers in lines of questioning that disrupt dominant ways of knowing. While digital tools might not achieve the personal connections we desire during coaching cycles, virtual video platforms offer us a practical way to engage in conversations that may have been somehow limited by the conventions of in-person meeting requirements.

During the observation, you can use a device to capture video of the teaching. This approach is tricky, however, because learners have the right to privacy. You need to be careful about capturing video that makes them vulnerable in various ways. We have, however, found that recording small moments can be valuable, if the learners are also protected if you use careful methods of recording, storing, and deleting data. Videos of classrooms are valuable in three main ways. You can slow down time and watch and rewatch clips to reflect on your teaching. Second, with virtual coaching, you can use videos to make the actual coaching sessions briefer: the participants can watch the video ahead of time, create reflective notes and action plans, and then spend a shorter time in dialogue during the postconference. Third, we know from our experiences during the pandemic that field supervisors were often unable to see the learners because of their limited access to the physical classroom. Using video that the teacher in the room collected was important to round out the field supervisor's understanding of the teaching and learning in the classroom.

Step 3. The Postconference

The postconference is often the part of the coaching cycle that generates knowledge about teaching and provides ample space for reflection. We recommend that any data collected during the observation be shared as soon as possible across the partnership. During the postconference, the role of each person depends on the role they took during the observation. Most important, the postconference should happen long enough after the observation so teachers have enough time to step away, study the data that were collected, and think and reflect.

The postconference will be time well spent when there is preparation. Again, figures 5.1–5.4 show how the opening question for a postconference will set the tone for the conversation. You may want to start with an open-ended question, too, such as "What have you been thinking about since the teaching event?" to provide each person with an opportunity to share their reflections. We have seen postconferences that are built from this opening question and do not depart from the topic. If one person was in a role of strictly observing, it is often better for that person to be a listener first, then prompting reflection or using data to draw out more observations and reflections. The person who was doing the teaching, in that case should be doing most of the talking. However, in a co-teaching scenario, you might find that each teacher will need time and a turn to share their thinking.

The postconference is often when coaching takes place. Coaching can take many forms, but as discussed in the next section, justice-focused coaching often takes up the hard questions around equity and access that are so important to our teaching. To get to this place, we have to be willing to enter into conversations that are sometimes difficult to start and, more so, difficult to maintain. The postconference must often be a place to ask each other questions such as, "What do you mean by that?" or "What data do we have that will help us to understand better?" One of our favorite coaching moves is the question "Can we slow down that moment?" With this request, we are asking a teacher to talk in detail about what they saw, heard, or experienced in the moment of teaching. Coaching means that we push each other to use the data we have collected to make sense of the teaching. You cannot accomplish everything in a postconference. Choosing an orientation to coaching can help you to narrow your focus toward justice and equity.

The postconference ends with an action plan, which has two parts. First, the coach and educator who was observed will want to ask each other, "Will something we understand about teaching and learning potentially apply to future activities, interactions, or lessons and have an impact on our teaching tomorrow, next week, or every day?" Action plans can be made for how a teacher might adapt a teaching method, adopt a change that was made, or approach interactions with a learner or a group. You can initiate the action plan with a phrase that feels comfortable to you and the other person, asking something like "So what are we taking into our teaching tomorrow (or every day)?" Second, the postconference action plan can include an intention for continuing the work together. Starting with a question such as "What might we do together or continue thinking about, in light of our conversation today?," you and your colleague can articulate how the partnership can continue over time as well.

PAUSE AND REFLECT

What are some coaching questions that stood out to you in this section? How might you include these in your next coaching cycle? What other questions would you add to your coaching tool kit?

Step 4. Planning

Planning is the closing of the loop from postconference to preconference. This step is not always feasible or even necessary, but we add it here as an option for you in justice-focused coaching. Planning is a time for extended dialogue and engagement with curriculum and instructional materials and methods. Planning is also discussed in detail in the book *Mentoring Preservice Teachers Through Practice: Coaching with CARE*. In that book, the coauthors define planning in the context of preservice teacher education and its value in teacher learning. More and more, we are seeing in-service teacher professional development that is curriculum-based and engages teachers in active inquiry around materials and practices.

During a planning period, we can even engage in rehearsals that might not be feasible in a preconference because of its short duration. In a rehearsal, one teacher tries out language or a practice with the other person observing. The observer can either role-play as a learner and provide feedback to the teacher from that position, or the observer can be a teaching partner, reflecting on the action with the other teacher. Rehearsals can be very useful in articulating the teaching moves that we hope to build in our practice.

HEATHER AND MADELYN'S STORY

As explained earlier, the case studies in this book are not meant to be exemplars or models but instead help explain the coaching tool being discussed. In this case, we share the story of one of us (Heather) and student teacher Madelyn. We look at their coaching cycle, the ways Heather drew on multiple orientations to coaching, and how she and Madelyn disrupted the dominant ways of knowing in the coaching cycle.

In the spring of 2020, Heather was working as field supervisor with Madelyn in a kindergarten class. Madelyn was in her second semester working with her cooperating teacher, Lori, and had utilized her time across both semesters to form strong relationships both with her cooperating teacher and with the learners in her classroom.

On a Wednesday morning, Heather pulled up to Mountain View Elementary for her weekly observation of Madelyn (coaching was happening face-to-face at this time). The school is located north of the metropolitan city, with a student demographic breakdown that is 52.2 percent White, 24.4 percent Hispanic, 12.5 percent Asian, 5.3 percent African American, and 5.1 percent two or more races. The ethnicity and race data are significant, because Madelyn was interested in how White students or Whiteness were centered in the classroom; she tried to choose texts that reflected the racial and ethnic demographics of learners in the classroom.

On Tuesday, Heather and Madelyn had a preconference about Madelyn's lesson. The teacher was planning on reading aloud a text, *Armadillo Rodeo* by Jan Brett, and focus on the characters, setting, problem, and solution of the story.[12] After reading the book aloud, Madelyn would guide the learners through their transition into small-group literacy stations: read to self, listen to reading, word work, and work on writing.[13] Madelyn and Heather, drawing on a humanistic orientation, decided in the preconference to collect data about a specific learner, Owen. Both Madelyn and Lori were puzzled by Owen's behaviors in the classroom and had decided to collect as much information as possible on his interactions during whole-group lessons. They would try to paint a clearer picture of what was going on, in hopes of supporting Owen and the other learners better during stations. Madelyn and Lori were aware of the amount of time Owen's behaviors were taking away from the rest of the class, but they also recognized that the learning environment was not meeting his needs. Not yet drawing on a critical perspective, Heather, as the field supervisor, saw this unique opportunity to provide an extra set of ears and eyes to take notes for Madelyn and Lori. Heather had two questions in the preconference: "What do we know about this specific community's needs and desires?" and "What would you like me to focus on in my observation? What data would you like me to collect?" Figure 5.6 includes these questions as well as the notes Heather recorded from their conversation.

FIGURE 5.6 *Applied observation tool: Justice-focused coaching cycle, preconference*

Observation date: ___ / ___ / ___	Who is present, and what are their roles?
	Heather, field supervisor
	Madelyn, teacher

Mode of observation (circle one):   (Live)   Video

Context (circle one):   **Co-teaching**   **Transparent observer**   (**Outside observer**)

Preconference discussion

• What do we know about this community's needs and desires?

Madelyn's inquiry project focuses on how teachers can help the learners who need extra support with social development skills. Specifically, she is interested in observing and thinking about one focal learner—Owen.

• What have we agreed to focus on today?

For this lesson, I will take detailed notes on Owen's behavior, thinking about both his interactions with the teacher and his interactions with his peers. What language is he using with his peers? When does he interrupt? Where is he physically positioned in the classroom? What are his nonverbal cues telling us?

At 8:15, the lesson began, and Heather sat in the back of the classroom, collecting notes on her laptop. She noted Owen's body language, his position on the rug, and his interaction with other learners. She also noted how Owen participated during the read-aloud, including asking clarifying questions about the text—"Why did they start to pinch?"—and seemingly off-topic comments like "I like your shoes. What about my shoes?"

At the end of the read-aloud, the learners moved into their reading stations. While Madelyn was working with a different group of learners, Heather began to turn her attention solely on Owen. At the word work station, Owen was trying his best to avoid a digraph sort by putting the cards in his mouth, dropping them to the floor, and standing up every couple of minutes to walk to the window. Heather noticed the potential mismatch between the learning environment and Owen's needs as a learner, and she began to think critically about this mismatch, given that Owen was identified as student with social-emotional needs unmet by the traditional teaching environment. She took a few notes on her laptop to prepare for the post-conference and then walked over to Owen's table. In the moment, Heather was thinking about Owen's avoidance of the learning experience and how his behaviors had begun to annoy his peers, as she recorded in figure 5.7.

FIGURE 5.7 *Applied justice-focused cycle observation tool: Reflections during observation*

Observational data	Reflections
What did you observe happening in the classroom related to community context and preconference goals?	Where might you affirm, wonder, or disrupt? What new questions do you have? Be specific.
OWEN: Why did they start to pinch? MADELYN: Because they were new. You know, sometimes when you have new shoes, they're tight. Because they get squished. OWEN: Yeah, you have to break them in.	This question tells me that Owen is following along with the read-aloud.
(During read-aloud.) OWEN *(Talks to the student next to him.)*: I like your shoes. What about my shoes?	Here it seems like Owen is trying to engage with his peer.
MADELYN: At the red table today during reading stations, you will be writing on this paper, and it's a story map. You will write about the setting, the characters. Who were the characters?	I wonder what prompted Owen to add "villain" into this word. Has the class been talking about villains within the story structure unit? Clever word play!

continues

FIGURE 5.7 *Continued*

Observational data	Reflections
What did you observe happening in the classroom related to community context and preconference goals?	Where might you affirm, wonder, or disrupt? What new questions do you have? Be specific.
CLASS: The armadillos. OWEN: The armavillains! They're villains. MADELYN: Then you'll write about the problem and the solution. STUDENT: What does that mean? MADELYN: How they solved the problem. MADELYN: Yes, Owen? OWEN: Armavillains.	
MADELYN: Owen, you're at the blue table, so you get to go to computers. OWEN: What are we supposed to be doing? MADELYN: Why don't you ask someone at your table? OWEN *(Shouts.)*: What is my password?	This seems likes a great redirect to see if Owen could seek help from his peers, but his response was to yell out instead.
OWEN *(Takes a picture card and then drops it on the floor.)*: No, this is the card for me! Can I eat it? Om nom nom nom nom. *(Owen is putting the card in his mouth.)* MADELYN: Owen, make sure that we don't put it on our mouth. That's how we spread germs, remember.	It feels like Owen is trying to avoid this activity.
(Owen throws another card on the ground.) *(Owen gets up frequently to look out the window.)* STUDENT: Owen, stop taking other people's work. OWEN: Zombie, zombie, zombie!	Here, Owen does not seem to acknowledge his peer's request to stop. The students at this center seem frustrated with Owen.

In light of these observations, Heather decided to move from an observer role to that of a co-teacher in the moment to engage Owen in the learning experience and model ways he could use his social emotional skills with his peers. Heather's orientation to coaching centered on the learners, and she realized she could learn more about Owen through these interactions. Heather's observation notes on the left of the figure and her comments and questions on the right indicate the specific moments when she was noticing and reflecting on Owen and his behavior and language.

As the small-group work time came to an end, Heather quickly went back to her laptop to capture the interaction with Owen. These notes then became a catalyst for conversation during the postconference. As Madelyn and Heather sat side by side, a physical move that positions both the teacher and the coach as collaborative peers, they looked carefully at the moments frozen in time by the observation notes. Having set the focus during the preconference, Madelyn and Heather returned to the questions they had generated about the focal learner. These questions came from a place of curiosity about him and a shared focus on equity in the classroom. Both women were concerned about Owen's learning and growth, asking questions such as "What are some of the causes of his behavior? Are his needs being met during whole-group activities?" Figure 5.8 represents the observation notes that Heather recorded after their conversation.

As a White child whose first language is English, Owen was a member of the racial majority of the classroom and the school. As Heather reflected on her conversation with Madelyn, she recognized the ways they both addressed issues of justice in their conversation, as well as the missed opportunities. For example, some learners in the classroom were learning English as a second language, and other students seemed to be less included in classroom conversations. Heather and Madelyn attended to critical orientations in their conversation, asking, "How does his behavior affect other learners'

FIGURE 5.8 *Applied justice-focused cycle observation tool: Postconference*

- What have you been thinking about since you taught the lesson?

  Madelyn reflected that considering the learners' good engagement with the text—their questions and answers about the book—the students were interested in this read-aloud.

  Madelyn wished she would have done a little better job explaining the characters and the setting during the whole-group instruction. By focusing on this step, she would have allowed for a more equitable experience for all the learners during their reading stations and would have made sure everyone understood these features in the text.

  How can we better explain characters and setting in kindergarten? Are there visual supports?

  Asking students about their writing project—making connections between reading and writing lessons

- (Specific planned questions based on observational data.)

  [Shared observation notes with Madelyn] What does this tell you about Owen as a learner? What questions are you still thinking about with him?

  His behaviors tend to be impulsive: his wanting to say something in the moment, wanting to get up from the table, etc. Madelyn is noticing how Owen is trying to interact with his peers, but the attempts often happen at nonideal moments (e.g., during the read-aloud or during workstation time). We might work with him on ways to interact with his peers in a way that would be helpful to both him and the other learners. How can we address this one-on-one? How can we build these social-emotional skills into our daily morning meetings?

---

learning experiences in the classroom?" Reflecting on these specific interactions with Owen allowed Madelyn and Heather to naturally move to problem-solving questions: "How can we design equitable learning experiences for Owen and the other learners in this classroom community?"

As we examine this case study, we wonder, though, How might Heather's coaching or her and Madelyn's conversations evolve to center on issues of race and Whiteness in a coaching cycle? Might this postconference have further explored how Owen's behavior in the classroom contributed to racial inequities in how students with diverse identities and ways of learning were included? The postconference conversation might naturally have led into additional conversations about curricula, instruction, and systems of inequality in schools.

For her student teaching inquiry project, Madelyn chose to focus on incorporating social-emotional skills into her daily morning meetings, with the intention of creating inclusive and restorative classroom communities. She also recruited Lori's support in hopes of teaching and modeling the skills that Owen and others would need, to empower them in their interpersonal relationships with their peers. While the subsequent observation cycles were not necessarily solely focused on Owen, Heather continued to check in with Madelyn and Lori on the ways they were working to support Owen and how their justice-focused social-emotional learning curriculum was going. By setting a focus in the preconference, collecting data during the observation, and reflecting together on these moments afterward, the justice-focused cycle served as a coaching tool where both the teacher and the coach could identify the pressing needs of the classroom community and work together toward justice in the classroom.

Roles, Responsibilities, and Power in This Story

Disrupting the expert–novice divide is sometimes more complex in the coaching cycle. The coach engages in focused observations and holds space for reflection through designated preconferences and postconferences. The teacher engages in these reflective moments before and after teaching. Roles and responsibilities can become very fixed in these structures. In this case, the defined roles and responsibilities were helpful in pushing Heather, as a coach, to use her designated space for reflection to focus on issues of race and equity in Madelyn's classroom.

A familiar power dynamic that Heather and Madelyn faced during their time together was that both women were ultimately visitors in

Lori's classroom, Heather more so than Madelyn. As a preservice teacher, Madelyn was welcomed into Lori's classroom during student teaching. However, Madelyn never held the full power of a classroom teacher in this space. Additionally, while Heather was a familiar visitor in the classroom, outside of the coaching cycles, she held little power in making changes to the curriculum and instruction. As a coach of preservice teachers, you may feel a certain familiarity in having conversations around what these teachers in training can do in a classroom. In these moments, we encourage both coaches and preservice teachers to work collaboratively with the classroom teachers. Like Madelyn, preservice teachers and coaches alike can invite classroom teachers into the coaching cycles or collaborative inquiry projects to work as a team toward justice-oriented goals.

CONCLUSION

In this chapter, we have built on earlier coaching tools to reframe the coaching cycle as a justice-focused coaching tool. This tool is perhaps the most ubiquitous approach in preservice and in-service teacher education. It is nimble enough to adjust to different orientations to coaching. It aims at disrupting expert–novice divides and engaging in broad notions of justice in community—the coach collaborates with the teacher to consistently integrate equity into their conversations in the pre- and postconference cycles. The coaching cycle is iterative, meaning it is repeated and tweaked to move a community closer to justice-focused practices that will lead to change. It may be overwhelming to think about how to hold these theoretical perspectives in mind and attend to the complex process of the justice-focused coaching cycle. This is why community is so important. We need each other so that we can give it a go, uncover problems, and solve them together.

As you embark on justice-focused coaching cycles, we encourage you to be patient with yourself and your community. There will be times when the postconference must be rescheduled because a parent needs to meet with you after school. Despite little setbacks, the tool is helping the community create the ripples of change they imagine. By keeping the reason for a coaching cycle clear in your mind, you will keep moving ahead. In the next chapter, we address how the expanded definitions of justice in communities will only deepen the impact of these coaching tools.

—— CHAPTER 6 ——

EMPATHY CONVERSATIONS

Throughout this book, we have described coaching tools for building communities that pursue justice in education together. We take a slight turn in these next two chapters, focusing on building and extending these communities to directly engage local contexts in our coaching. Empathy conversations are planful conversations designed to build relationships based on stakeholder experience. This tool demands that the coaching participants step outside coaching's traditional field of vision (the classroom and the lesson) to bring more voices to the table and more stories to frame the coaching so that teachers throughout the school can focus directly on community.

Gerald Campano and his colleagues acknowledge the labor involved in "fostering empathy and inclusivity" and, in fact, recognize it as a vital component of interdependence and horizontal expertise.[1] They use words such as *symbiotic, recursive, ongoing,* and *fluid* to describe the mutual, active labor of healthy and trusting community-based inquiry. Moreover, their recognition of labor is particularly noteworthy in relation to expanding communities for coaching; breaking the expert–novice barrier requires significant labors of learning and unlearning.

People's positions in each empathy conversation will vary according to differences in power, identities, roles, and purposes. What cannot vary, however, is the intentionality and care a person must apply when handling other people's stories. They must exert great care when making claims and taking actions that can shape lives. We will urge you throughout this chapter to seek a multiplicity of voices to undertake your decision-making. In this chapter, we'll show how you can use empathy conversations to understand the experiences of colleagues, learners, and families to expand your local knowledge of your community. We also address how this collective voice can then be used as within coaching toward building race-conscious and justice-oriented practices. After learning some practical tools, you'll also hear how one of us (Kerry) led an equity committee at Southwest Elementary, a school in a large urban district. Besides being an author, Kerry also identifies as a curious and invested parent and educator on this campus.

PAUSE AND REFLECT

Let's get started right away. Take out your journal and begin to make a list of the people in the community or communities you are a part of. As you think of who is in your community, are there particular relationships you would like to grow or strengthen? Highlight or star those names. Where are your relationships already strong? Mark those as well. Share your list with others you are working with as you continue to expand your list.

BACKGROUND: WHAT ARE EMPATHY CONVERSATIONS?

Empathy conversations are an offshoot of the larger group of approaches we can call empathy or user interviews. Empathy interviews have been used across industries to elicit user experiences in organizations and to identify aspects of the organization in need of improvement. Most recently, projects in design thinking have drawn on empathy interviews to get a sense of the user experience.[2] Additionally, the Carnegie Foundation for the Advancement of Teaching strongly advocates empathy interviews as a cornerstone of improvement science work as part of a theory of systems and how they might be changed.[3] We honor this history and propose a set of practices that align with justice-focused coaching.

Relationship Building and Interrupting the Traditional Expert–Novice Divide

To center relationship building, we intentionally replaced the term *interview* with *conversation* in our use of this tool, as an interview elicits some of the features of power we endeavor to change. When someone is interviewed, the roles are well established. One person asks the questions; the other person provides the answers. Even semistructured and ethnographic interviews maintain this directional focus.[4] Interviews draw on a history of research that has brought great harm to BIPOC communities. Interviewers often assume they are gathering objective data rather than participating in a social event with the interviewee. Scholars often present the results from interview studies as objective data, rather than contextualizing the interview as a social event mediated by the identities of those involved in the interview. Moreover, interviewees can be exposed to harm by questions that are painful or emotional. Unlike an interview, a conversation is an occasion for the participants to discuss common interests. The term takes us out of defined roles about who holds the questions and whose knowledge or talk is being elicited. A conversation is relational and positions both parties as change agents. However, we cannot just change the name to *conversation* and expect harm to be mitigated. Therefore, we include the term *empathy* as well as *conversation* to describe this tool.

Empathy conversations can elevate voices that are often missing in key conversations and decision-making meetings or events. This aspect of empathy conversations relates to the double meaning of justice-focused coaching. When you learn about and understand the knowledge and experience of one another, you can understand how people experience systems differently because of their racial and ethnic identities, their gender and sexuality, their status in the organization (student, staff member, paraprofessional, etc.), the languages they speak, and so on. In this sense, empathy conversations would be likely to uncover the ways that racism, gender normativity, sexism, xenophobia, and other oppressions are occurring in the system. These conversations are valuable when conducted across an organization so that we can also understand the differences in how people experience the system.

More than Sympathy: A Tool for Finding Connection

Brené Brown often talks about "holding space" for others, or the ability to listen, to withhold judgment or interpretation, as a way of honoring another's humanity.[5] She differentiates empathy from sympathy; empathy builds connection because it is a way of being with the other, not solving the problem or feeling badly for the other. Empathy is what you might experience when someone shares an experience and you take it in completely, searching for a connection. For example, a child in your classroom experienced a letdown, and you remembered the feeling of disappointment in your own body so well that you almost experienced their response yourself. Or perhaps you asked someone about a recent experience, providing them the opportunity to talk at length about what it felt like for them. Both of these scenarios are examples of practicing empathy.

What kinds of questions in a conversation lend themselves to empathy and connection? We will get you started here, but there is no right answer. In fact, empathy conversations will differ across communities, because the ways of sharing and norms of conversations differ across communities. For one community, you might consider questions like "What was it like to be a new teacher at this school?" or "What do you like best about the school schedule? What is challenging for you about the school schedule?" For another community, it may be more appropriate to use story-eliciting questions, such as "Can you tell me about a time when . . . ?" The kinds of questions that are less favored would be closed questions (those that merely require a yes-or-no answer) or questions that seek information like, "What is the school schedule this year?" Open-ended questions are focused on a person's experience of a system, not about the system itself. Only by focusing on experience can we challenge the narratives that schools are equitable and caring for all learners.

Table 6.1 is an example of a conversation structure we developed for work with our university's cohort coordinators and mentor teachers. We then revised this structure for conversations with other stakeholders, such as caregivers.

Recognizing the Significance of Identities, Histories, and Power

An empathy conversation relates to both the individual connections we make and the ways that empathy can build as we engage with media, stories, literature, and other texts that widen our understanding of experiences different from our own. Empathy can refer to having practices to hear and understand how some people's experiences are shaped by violent and oppressive beliefs. One way to think about empathy is in relation to racism and xenophobia. The belief that English-speaking Americans, and those who are socially constructed as White, are linguistically, intellectually, and emotionally superior to other Americans can be found in every institution, including schools, banks, and medical establishments.

White people often resist hearing and believing stories of racism. Although White people's popular knowledge of interpersonal or blatant racism is strong (and they find it easy to deny their complicity in this form of racism), their understanding of institutional or systemic racism is often underdeveloped. Zeus Leonardo and other scholars who examine Whiteness have documented how those who have historically and contemporarily benefited from beliefs and practices about race that disadvantage BIPOC have difficulty examining systemic racism.[6] To practice empathy, we must be aware of the history

TABLE 6.1 *Designing the empathy conversation: Reflective questions to consider together*

Warmup Choose a question that allows for connection	• What [color, flower, animal] represents your emotions today? Why? • What made you feel capable in your work today? • If you could rewind your day to 6 a.m., what would you do differently?
Set a purpose	*Example*: "There are two reasons I wanted to talk with you today. One is I am hoping we can get to know each other better as [teachers, other roles] to strengthen our work together. Also, I hope that we can get to know our [system, school, program] better by hearing each other's experiences."
About the individual	• How did you come to be a [teacher, caregiver, etc.] at [location]? • Will you share with me what it is like to be a [role] at [location] or a member of [community organization]? • What is a time when you felt impactful and happy in your [position, membership]? What are you proud about? • What challenges do you face as a [role] most often? • Can you describe what kinds of interactions and experiences you have on a typical day at this school? • What do you think of most when you're not at school?
Histories of teaching and learning	• What changes has this community pursued over time? • What has worked well for this community in working toward change? What has been challenging?
Focusing on inequities	• What are the inequities we see happening in [your classroom, our school, our program, our community]? • Which practices in our classroom or school are ripe for interruption and revision in terms of inequities? • What have we done to address those inequities in our community? How did it go?

and reach of these benefits, or White privilege, and position ourselves to act to disrupt it. We must also be willing to hear, and learn about, theories that may be unsettling to our worldview. In a valuable article about empathy and White teachers, Chezare Warren reminds us that for these teachers, empathy requires a deep engagement with the experiences of families and learners of Color.[7] He says that there is plenty of evidence in the literature that what we think of as empathy is often false and is actually used to alleviate a White person's guilt or, worse, to reward the White person for their efforts toward helping. To be in community, we need to be conscious of how we interpret what we hear and why we sometimes have difficulty holding space for others' stories.

For coaches who identify as BIPOC, we note that empathy is a racialized construct, and the idea of holding space for the other's humanity may have at times been harmful to you. Indeed, holding space is not always safe. As White people and the authors of this book, we are careful not to suggest that our own experiences of empathy conversations involve the same kinds of risks that our colleagues often take. When conversations with others are harmful and hurtful, every human has the right to decline to participate. We do not intend to suggest that harmful and violent interactions can be tolerated if they are pursued under the veil of empathy. It is crucial that before entering this work, we take stock of our own histories, identities, and resources for entering vulnerable spaces with others.

PAUSE AND REFLECT

Stop and journal a bit about these ideas of identities, histories, and power. Think of the questions in table 6.2 as your groundwork for entering empathy conversations with colleagues and other stakeholders.

TABLE 6.2 *Groundwork for empathy conversations: Journal questions*

Experiences around empathy	• Think about a time you remember having difficulty practicing empathy. What identities, roles, or lack of information may have gotten in the way of your connecting and understanding in that moment? • Think of a time when empathy came easier for you. • What is different about this moment? How do your intersecting identities play a role? Did the context play a role?
Perceived differences	• How might your own experiences with empathy differ from those of others in your school or community?

continues

TABLE 6.2 *Continued*

Comfort versus discomfort	• Think about the list you made at the beginning of this chapter. Who on that list is someone you could enter into an empathy conversation with, genuinely wanting to understand? What would make this a comfortable conversation? • Who do you feel less prepared to talk with, and why?
Opportunities to grow	• What thoughts and feelings do you have about using empathy conversations as part of your practice? • What are ways you can redesign how you spend time together with others in your community to focus more on stories that have been denied because of the urgency of schooling?

Next, we will discuss how power is related to your roles and responsibilities in empathy conversations.

Power in Institutional Roles

Planning for and conducting empathy conversations takes social, relational strength—the conversations require meaningful and purposeful labor. And the work is not easy, especially if the coach is new to the role and the community or if the teachers being coached are not already familiar with the campus ethos and local power dynamics. It is here where responsible teachers make relationship building and learning about the community a priority. Also, if you can ask for an empathy conversation, it is likely you hold some institutional power. If you are a student teacher or a novice teacher, think about the power that comes with being a newcomer in this space, even though you may often feel like you have less power. If someone reaches out and says, "Let me know if you need anything as you get settled in," honor that invitation! If you have more institutional power, such as an administrative position, think about how you show respect to those who have less institutional power. Check your assumptions about power; assumptions have no place in coaching for justice.

If you are in the role of coach, it is important that you help a community take up empathy conversations together. You do not need to be the one initiating all the conversations, nor do you need to always be present. You might take on a role to support others. You might become a coach or a facilitator, particularly in the design of the empathy conversations (e.g., facilitating a group empathy conversation) and during the analysis. Before beginning to coach, you will find it helpful to think about how coaching typically supplements practice and depends on your own reflections about your capacity to do the work and having the necessary tools. We expand this idea later in the book, as coaches have a key role in facilitating shared inquiry.

The following "How can you?" questions will help you puzzle through the roles, responsibilities, and power dynamics that might arise when you are planning for or conducting empathy conversations. This work will lay the groundwork for shared inquiry, a topic covered later in the book.

How can you prepare as a coach to encourage a community to use empathy conversations?

- Reflect on your role in the community and the potential ways to be supportive. You might want to ask the community members, "Who else?" as they are deciding on who to include in conversations and continuing to discover who can be part of the empathy conversations to expand what can be learned.
- Consider whether you want to facilitate the conversation, watch and listen, or take notes. Listening can be powerful— you may find ways to bring emerging patterns to the surface during the conversations or to ask probing questions to follow-up on ideas beginning to emerge, as we will show in our case study.

What might you need to consider or do before and during an empathy conversation?

- Take a moment to breathe. Center yourself and review your intentions. You are building relationships that will guide your work, in your community. That is your North Star.
- Time and mental and physical bandwidth are precious resources in schooling communities. Invite stakeholders into conversations with grace and compassion, and make sure to stick to prearranged time frames. Show up. Be present. Leave distractions at home.
- Keep a close eye on how certain identities or perspectives get re-centered because of who is chosen to be part of the conversation. Be aware of these roles and histories.
- Think about the power you hold in your own institutional role and how you might have to question assumptions about power in this process.

How can you honor the participants in empathy conversations in ways that lead to sustained relationships?

- Be mindful of reciprocity. What are *you* bringing (or what have you brought) to this space? What labors can you or will you provide? How will your work support the work of the community writ large?
- Reserve some time after each conversation to reflect on the experience. What did you learn, and what stories were told? Identify how you will honor the consent, privacy and boundaries set by your colleagues, the caregivers, or other partners within these collaborations.
- After your conversations, support the participants by identifying the patterns in the data, and guide them on the use of

theory as a lens to analyze the data. Continue asking what other voices need to be heard if you are to understand the range of perspectives on this issue.

EMPATHY CONVERSATIONS: A PRACTICAL GUIDE

As we have done with the previous coaching tools, we now offer you practical suggestions for having empathy conversations. Some of these steps will seem repetitive if you have already been working with other coaching tools. However, if you are jumping in right here—and you might be doing so, depending on your community and role—we'll start with identifying your community and then expanding the community to include new voices and perspectives.

Empathy conversations typically last no more than thirty to sixty minutes and are often conducted in person (when possible) to allow for all the participants to experience people's body language, personhood, and emotions. Although virtual environments can be good platforms for empathy conversations, these communication tools are more effective in person. Empathy conversations are a recursive process: each step leads to the next (figure 6.1).

Step 1. Identify Your Community

As discussed, the first step is to identify your community and then expand it. Learning communities can constitute very large groups, such as a university's teacher preparation program that leads to initial certification. They can also be smaller communities, such as an inquiry group supporting teachers' work for social change in the classroom. A community might be a fourth-grade team analyzing assessment results and plans for curricula. It is important to understand communities learning together when embarking on new initiatives. Here, you will need to think within the scope of the practices that are ripe for interruption and revision: you'll be thinking about your community

FIGURE 6.1 *Recursive nature of empathy conversations*

in relation to the inequities you hope to address. You may want to revisit your work in chapter 2 to identify your spheres of influence.

If you are an educator who is working alone on this project of developing your practice, you might think of empathy conversations as a tool for recruiting a community for your professional growth. Consider how the perspectives in the empathy conversations will stretch your own viewpoint and those of others.

Empathy conversations may begin as a single scheduled event, but the conversations will probably continue as the relationships and collaborations become more familiar. For example, perhaps you aimed to have an empathy conversation with each of the school's mentor teachers, and over the year, the conversations continued. Collaborating on problems of practice, in this case, would multiply the voices and experiences available for designing equitable instruction. Shared inquiry questions about decentering Whiteness in the fourth-grade social studies curriculum needs many minds and eyes on materials and, most importantly, time to critically examine and debrief with colleagues and peers. Building relationships in this way reminds us that education is a collective endeavor that benefits from multiple voices. Not every empathy conversation will lead to inquiry work or peer coaching, but common interests often emerge from these conversations.

Step 2. Design the Empathy Conversation

Once you have identified the *who* of your conversations, you will design the discussions to build relationships and the capacity for justice-focused coaching. Working together to design these conversations is an ideal way to create an event that will reflect a shared vision of what all of you want to accomplish in the conversations.

As you may recall, table 6.1 summarizes the questions we call warmup (first round), setting a purpose (second round), individual focus (third round), histories of teaching and learning (fourth round), and areas for inquiry (last round). During the warmup, you check in on your feelings and emotional state before beginning the conversation. This is also a time for introductions if the conversation is happening with strangers or new acquaintances. You might think about pulling the questions that speak to you and your context from each section, to choose your own adventure in the conversation. To position both or all people as learners, you might want to take turns answering questions. Empathy conversations should have a set ending, and the participants should be encouraged to think through how they might move forward together when they have more time to talk and work.

You want to show appreciation for the time all of you have spent together and for everyone's willingness to share and be vulnerable, and you will want to plan or commit to further the conversation.

In addition, technology might support the empathy conversation in a few ways. First, technology can take on the role of facilitator, taking this responsibility off the plate of a single participant in the conversation. For example, when working online with a class of preservice teachers and their mentors, we created a Jamboard with individual pages for each question in our empathy conversation, and mentors and preservice teachers posted their responses in real time to the questions before engaging in a discussion. The questions were focused on the transition to online teaching and co-teaching during Covid: "What are you most excited to try in your teaching?" and "What concerns do you have about co-teaching virtually?" The Jamboard did not replace the conversation but instead functioned as a *quick write* to quickly gather thinking and responses before the live Zoom discussion that was focused on the inquiry and justice orientations of the teacher education program. The Jamboard took the place of a facilitator or an interviewer who held the questions in their hand.

You must also have a way to collect what you learn during the empathy conversation. Here are some ideas that are on the continuum of more to less labor-intensive tools for collecting people's input. We have found it to be useful and humanizing to have a recording to hear the voices of those we have interviewed, but sometimes the act of recording could limit what people will say. Therefore, we recommend having a conversation together about whether recordings will be useful and their potential costs and benefits. Figure 6.2 shows the range of ways you can collect input from an empathy conversation. For example, you can use a template like the conversation reflection template in table 6.3 to collect your reactions either during or after the empathy conversation.

FIGURE 6.2 *Continuum for collecting input in a conversation*

More labor-intensive	←————————→	Less labor-intensive
Record the conversation using Zoom or another video conferencing software program. Many of these programs have an auto-transcription capability, which you can use to refer to the conversation.	Use your smartphone to record the conversation as you talk. On your question sheet, note or highlight the places you want to come back to and listen to again.	Use a template (e.g., the one in table 6.3) to write down what you hear and feel and your questions and ideas for the next action steps.

Step 3. Conduct an Analysis

After the empathy conversation, you'll ideally want to do some processing of the conversation. You can do this in groups or individually. Depending on the method you chose to collect the conversation, you'll

TABLE 6.3 *Reflection template for empathy conversations*

Participants and date:	Purpose of the conversation:
What did you *hear*?	What were your initial *impressions*?
What *questions* do you have?	What *action steps* are next?

want to approach the analysis a little differently. If you used Zoom or another platform to automatically record and transcribe the conversation, you might take some time to read through the transcription and jot down anything that relates to your goals for the conversation. If you made an audio recording, you could similarly relisten to the conversation and make some notes. Here, the template we suggested for note-taking might be helpful.

The empathy conversations you conduct should guide future inquiry work and coaching that is, as we will discuss later, focused on shared inquiry. Therefore, you may want to do some analysis of empathy conversations conducted within a system. Compile your notes, and look for some themes—some clues—about what is most important across this community. Think about the practices that people name again and again as examples of justice, or injustice, on the campus. The key in this step is how we have chosen to have conversations with people who represent a range of perspectives, to get to the roots of our shared history and to initiate (or sustain) a broader community relationship.

Step 4. Reflect into Coaching

Once you have recorded and analyzed your conversation data, you must spend time reflecting on your notes before you move into coaching. Figure 6.3 represents the mindfulness we expect when engaging with people's stories. You may add or revise the prompts in the figure according to your own situation, but we suggest using these as a starting point. You can do this work individually or collectively to process the relational data with respect and to strategically plan for shared inquiry, justice-focused coaching cycles, and actively observing practice together.

Next, we will consider the empathy conversations that one of us (Kerry) and the community had for the purpose of developing an equity committee at Southwest Elementary.

FIGURE 6.3 *Reflect into coaching*

What is shared?

- A personal story
- A hope
- A frustration
- A concern

What must be considered?

- Have I expressed gratitude?
- Whose story is this to tell?
- Have I sought consent from the speaker to engage with this story? Is so, how would the speaker like to proceed?
- What themes (systemic, institutional) are embedded in this concern?
- How do race, power, and context show up in this theme?
- Whose safety and privacy need to be prioritized?

What next?

- Consider how this theme shows up in curricular materials, on wall spaces, between learners and colleagues.
- Monitor the presence of this theme in planning, collect questions as they arise.
- Learn more about this theme in the local context. Who in your sphere of influence might know more about this theme?
- Consider engaging a shared inquiry.

KERRY'S STORY

Tucked between a busy crossroad and a growing cluster of apartment homes, townhomes, and single-family homes, Southwest Elementary serves around six hundred children from nearby working- to middle-class families. The population is 41 percent Hispanic, 41 percent White, 7 percent Asian, 7 percent two or more races, 3 percent Black, 0.5 percent American Indian, and 0.2 percent Pacific Islander; one-third of the children receive free or reduced-price lunch.[8]

To foster a broader network of support and local knowledge, Kerry, as a parent, field supervisor, and former teacher at the elementary campus, purposefully joined the PTA to assume the role of equity chair. Motivated by her commitment to the students in the school and the culturally sustaining goals of the teacher education program, the committee used a book study, choosing *Belonging Through a Culture of Dignity* to develop a collective vision of justice between parents, teachers, and school leaders.[9] This book had been recommended by a district cultural proficiency and inclusiveness specialist, as it was one the specialist's own team would be using to ground their work in the coming year. Then, for two years, the committee conducted empathy conversations to shape community practices toward equity and racial justice. Of particular interest to the group was shifting the discourses of Whiteness in the schooling ethos over the years. Kerry thought that aligning resources with district leadership would provide a wealth of shared language when the school community would engage complex race-equity issues. Not only this, but the word *belonging* felt key to the group's goal of acknowledging power dynamics (and consciously working to minimize them) to protect all stakeholders and maintain their sense of trust.

Steps 1 and 2. Identify Your Community, and Design the Conversation

For two years, Kerry met with families, teachers, staff, and administrators in monthly gatherings. At these meetings, both in person and on Zoom during the pandemic, stakeholders took the time to share community concerns, critically examine and cowrite local documents such as vision statements and letters of support and engage in boundary-crossing discourse around equity-centered articles and media. Table 6.4 shows some of the questions Kerry initially used to draw more community voices into her coaching and teaching of preservice teachers around race-equity issues.

TABLE 6.4   *Example questions and comments to start an empathy conversation*

Campus teachers	A few of our preservice teachers are on the same elementary campus for their internships, but they rarely get a chance to interact with other professionals besides their own cooperating teacher Different teacher mentors may have different experiences with similar tensions about race or equitable instruction in this community. Do these teachers have stories that might reframe our perspective on various inquiry topics? For example, does their social studies curriculum center on Whiteness, or does it take a more justice-focused approach? And how do they do this?
Assistant principal	I know the assistant principal has a broad-lens perspective on the school faculty. She would be a great resource for our inquiry projects this semester. For example, who on campus does she know who is incorporating the science of teaching reading with a culturally relevant lens? Who is engaged in student-centered math instruction? And how does she feel our preservice teachers can be supportive in return?
Principal	The principal has been a great advocate for families this year since Covid-19 and transitioning in and out of virtual learning. What is his pulse on the community since returning to face-to-face instruction? What tensions around equity are shaping his (and his teachers') decision-making? How does he feel we can be most supportive to the families and teachers at the school at this time?
Caregivers and other family members	I know the school has an equity committee as part of its PTA. I'd love to join. I could learn more from the handful of parents and caregivers and ask who might be willing to visit and speak about their own experiences. I could ask what kinds of literacy projects and other practices the parents wish to see in their children's classrooms. I could also ask more questions about what kinds of literacy practices the families engage in at home
Afterschool care counselors	Many of our preservice teachers' learners attend afterschool programs on the campus. This could be a great opportunity to learn more about the learners outside of the classroom. What are their interests?

Empathy conversations do not happen in a vacuum: Kerry embedded empathy conversations in a range of activities the equity committee undertook to build shared understandings and orientations toward justice. Here, we begin with a summary of some of these efforts.

Kerry committed to spending time at Southwest Elementary. She listened to teachers, parents, caregivers, and administrators communicate their concerns and celebrations. As she began taking an active role in race-equity community discussions, stakeholders began reaching out to her as a thinking partner around issues of equity and schooling—a sign of growing reciprocity. During long periods of virtual learning, for example, when parents were privy to the goings-on in classrooms in new ways, certain traditional practices came under new scrutiny. New questions erupted, such as "What is the value of turning cameras on all day? What if I hear something that makes me uncomfortable?"

One Black parent, Alice, called Kerry on the phone to discuss what she thought were biased comments she had overheard in her child's classroom. Because of the sensitive nature of the issue, Kerry, with Alice's permission, brought these concerns to the equity committee. At the time, there was no guide for families to express race-equity concerns in a way that felt safe and comfortable. For some families, schooling memories are rife with harm and anxiety, and speaking up can reify a similar trauma response. Together with the administration and teachers, the committee cowrote and published on the school website a schoolwide callout titled "Invitation to Dialogue." This piece of shared writing, which provided counselor information, committee information, and district information, represented a step in widening the opportunity and audience with whom to share story.

Months later, Alice invited Kerry to coffee at a local bakery to check in. They discussed the changes they'd seen in the way the school was operating regarding community voice. Although there were still biases and barriers embedded in the system, it was clear that the stories caregivers and learners shared were being honored, discussed, and negotiated in new ways. This change, Alice noted, was a significant shift from when her son had attended the same school. In this case, Kerry and Alice used empathy to shape larger decisions about how the school could listen more attentively to its families.

Step 3. Conduct an Analysis

As we discussed in this chapter, Kerry, as a coach in this community, began to ask herself what patterns were emerging in the stories she heard as stakeholders were also becoming more familiar with each other's goals and intentions. For Kerry's purposes toward racial equity, she reviewed the notes and agendas from the most recent two years of community conversations and looked for any clues to how and where conversations fostered change and led to inquiry and action. Through (trust-centered) storytelling, she began to see how it was the children's lived experiences at the school, as told through caregiver and teacher voices, that most directly shaped community inquiry and action. For example, one parent's story describing implicit biases on campus led four White teachers to begin a book study on Whiteness and anti-racism. Another parent's story prompted the school to host local authors Bavu Blakes and Ellison Blakes to support schoolwide social-emotional learning initiatives. Their book, *El's Mirror*, became a schoolwide mentor text on the importance of listening to one another.[10] By conducting empathy conversations in monthly meetings, Kerry's committee collectively targeted schoolwide practices and elicited horizontal expertise on a variety of equity concerns. Notably, the committee had conversations with people who represented a range of perspectives, to get to the roots of the group's shared history and to initiate (or sustain) a broader community relationship.

To provide some examples of what empathy conversations sound like, we now take you inside some conversations from the elementary equity committee's monthly work and Kerry's analysis of those conversations. Kerry invited a few regular attendees of the group to meet one-on-one to see how the concept of the equity varied across different roles and perspectives. Not everyone in the group had experience as an educator, but everyone made a significant investment in the well-being of the whole. The following segments will highlight two voices in particular, Mr. B., the school principal, and Carmen, a parent of two elementary learners. In the first example, we share the nuances of how Kerry navigated the conversation with Mr. B. as a facilitator. In the second example, we highlight the record keeping and analysis Kerry used to make sense of the conversation with Carmen.

KERRY AND MR. B.'S EMPATHY CONVERSATION

KERRY (FACILITATOR, PARENT, COACH): In retrospect [of the past two years], where have you felt personal struggle, or had to grow, with the community work?

MR. B. (SCHOOL PRINCIPAL): I think the trusting-relationships piece [stretched me], because in relational work, you have to make yourself vulnerable. But again . . . I am the principal of our campus, so [as a principal] you have to make yourself vulnerable but also recognize the position of power that you sit in.

Kerry's questions were framed around the school PTA's equity work over two years. Mr. B., a new principal at the committee's outset, readily attended monthly meetings, helped to cowrite a shared vision statement, and encouraged open dialogue among caregivers, teachers, and staff. He began the conversation in recognition of his positionality and how relational and institutional negotiations shaped his participation.

MR. B.: So, balancing that out. It goes back to how much time we have, and [incorporating] new things like HB 4545 for example.[11] And yes, there are things about that [legislation] that can connect with equity work. But then there's also parts of that that are very time-consuming, just extra time-consuming, and kind of managerial. Next year we'll have the sixty hours of reading academies required.

KERRY: Okay. (*Nods.*) Yeah, I know about that.

MR. B.: Yeah, so you know, that's our teachers in kindergarten through third. And myself, I will have to do that . . . And it's like, you want our equity work to be at the forefront, but then, you also have to incorporate new policy, so you have to look at it [and ask yourself], "How do I incorporate these pieces, but then also, how do I balance it?" And part of it is like, "All right, what are the steps that we can take?"

The questions Kerry posed allowed Mr. B. to share some challenges he experienced when navigating his roles as school principal (and district representative) with that of a responsive community leader. His use of words like *balance* and *incorporate* signified a generative laboring toward equitable decision-making. By partnering the words *time-consuming* and *managerial*, he showed how demands of office work took precedence, rather than the community work he preferred to do, when these responsibilities piled up. This recognition of the labor Mr. B. was taking on led Kerry to ask about specific ways he found footing when he was integrating new policy or district initiatives. Time, it seems, and how he attended to it, were clues to the broader community culture.

KERRY: It does feel like you, by showing up [to the gatherings] . . . like you and I show up, a few other people show up . . . we are prioritizing how we spend our time. Can you name places, specifically, where tensions erupt with how you're aligning with equity work? Like you mentioned before about the reading academies—how do you negotiate equity work with that new policy?[12]

MR. B.: One of the things I wrestle with is, and I think we all do as educators (when I was assistant principal and now as principal) is [that] every day, when I step into this building, there are eight hours of things, or more, that I have to do, that need to be done, sitting at my computer in the office. But all the meaningful work that needs to happen, like being out engaging with students, engaging with staff, modeling things for staff . . . the time you spend doing that pushes the other eight hours of computer work to the evening. . . . And I think the most powerful opportunities for equity comes from being out there, seeing something, being able to respond to it immediately or use it as a teachable moment. But if you're not out there interacting, then you're going to miss out on those opportunities. It's keeping a pulse on that balance; I think it's a constant struggle all of us educators are wrestling [with].

KERRY: Totally. No one tells you that when you first go in [to education], your whole life, you're going to feel like you're being kind of torn in half, in that way.

At the time of this conversation, the tensions Mr. B. described, including the need to incorporate new policies and the increasing paperwork, were couched in Covid-19 politics and palpable campuswide exhaustion with the weight of it all. Additionally, rather than repeating questions, Kerry practiced empathy by following Mr. B.'s lead. She recognized the exhaustion felt by most educators in the current climate and the need for many hands and voices in the pursuit of equity in schooling spaces. She welcomed pauses to allow him to expand these ideas and say more.

KERRY: So, at the end of the day . . . how do you gauge how the community [at large] feels about your work? How do you know if you're doing it well?

MR. B.: I think it's a lot of different ways. You have things as formal as the [district] surveys are going out that provide feedback. Sometimes it's phone calls and conversations, sometimes it's connecting in an ARD [Admission, Review, and Dismissal] meeting, and a parent provides you some direct feedback, positive [ideas], or areas for growth. Some of it is with [a districtwide communication system via school websites], for example, so it's very accessible for families to communicate if they have concerns or if needs are not being met. I think when we reach out to families and connect with them in different ways, with honesty and with comfort, they'll share. And I think that if you're experiencing that the communication is closed off, it's a big reflective point, like, "Okay, we don't have a relationship there to work off. What do we need to do differently to connect in some way?" So, yeah, that's a big piece, and with our work and goals is that piece of, like, "I'm one person, you're one person."

At this moment in the conversation, Mr. B. was on a roll. Kerry nodded to acknowledge his understanding of restorative practices and how "we" as educators and, more specifically, he as principal cannot restore a relationship that had never existed in the first place. She was keen to not interrupt or turn the conversation but to let him expand further.

MR. B. (CONTINUING): For example, the land acknowledgment was one of the things [a staff member] was really pushing. She was like, "Hey, I want you to come share this at our first faculty meeting." And yet if I do it, it might be like, "Oh, this is Mr. B.'s thing," and "He's going to make us do this," and then you might get people just following it because, like, you tell them to do that, whereas I don't . . . That's why I loved when y'all were able to do the book club last year. For [the teachers] to be able to feel comfortable doing it, and I don't have to be there, because, as you know from being a teacher, even with the best administrators, how much time am I in your individual classroom? How many interactions do I really get to see? So, you know, if we don't build that up within our teachers and our staff, then it's not going to happen consistently, because I'm one person working eighty hours a week most weeks, and I can't do all of it.

KERRY: Yes, we need more spring break. (*Laughs.*)

Mr. B. addressed these concerns about equity by using his own role as an example. He showed how particular events, such as teacher-led book clubs, either supported his vision of strong equitable leadership and faculty development or, because of the managerial workload, thwarted his ability to "do it all."

MR. B.: How can we provide courageous spaces [while also recognizing that] the challenge right now is the exhaustion piece? How can we continue to build up everyone's capacity? Because we can't just be one person or two people or three people . . . It's got to be everybody.

One notable recurrence in Mr. B's language is his use of "we" when he was discussing the committee's work. We hear in his responses how the construct of *principal* (the role as broadly defined by the system) repeatedly positions and repositions his energies and intentions toward leader-as-autocrat, whereas he clearly believes the community's well-being is a labor of many.

Each of Kerry's follow-up questions centered on what she heard Mr. B. saying, showing that she was focused on empathy in this interview. Kerry and Mr. B. have spent time in similar community conversations over the years; their involvement has built a foundation of trust—a vital component when people are discussing issues that cross sociocultural and political boundaries. As White educators and teacher leaders, both Kerry and Mr. B. recognize that their racial and professional identities hold a particular sway depending on who they are in conversation with. In fact, knowing how Whiteness shapes systems and dialogue, therefore, remains key to relational affinity, planning, and reflection. In closing, Mr. B. named how he had changed because of the continuing collaboration between families, teachers, and the school system:

KERRY: Looking back, can you think of an activity or an event or tool that changed your perspective? Or something that really struck you?

MR. B.: I think the biggest thing has been individuals, different people, sharing their stories and the way things have impacted them. Like intent versus impact, where someone will share something that impacts them in a negative way, and then [you are] stopping, reflecting, like, "Oh!" That just opens your eyes. I think that grows us in our work, because, one, we can hopefully address that specific situation, but then, later on, build your tool kit as someone committed to equity work; we can stop and be like "Oh, remember that one time, where we weren't thinking about this? How can I incorporate that in this decision we're about to make?"

The empathy conversation helped Kerry understand some of the structural issues and state policies that affected the equity committee's ability to create change on the elementary campus. Although

Mr. B. shared quite a lot, he was careful to protect the privacy and confidentiality of concerns with which he'd been entrusted. This is an important challenge for justice-focused educators to remember: as public-facing community members, we put relationships first—not everyone's story will be told to *you*, but everyone's story deserves to be told. It is not our right to know all things; rather, it is our responsibility to recognize the whole. We may not embody the identities of our colleagues and families in our care, but the safety and inclusivity of each are our responsibility.

The conversational moves Kerry made with Mr. B. were grounded in empathy and geared toward understanding his concepts of (and experiences with) equity in his role as principal, the local circumstances, and the current climate. Broadly, Kerry was mindful about listening deeply and allowed for generative pauses. She didn't repeat questions, and though it's not evident in this transcript, she passed over some questions she had anticipated asking. The stories and reflections Mr. B. shared were the ones closest to his thinking at that moment, and these are the active details that Kerry wanted to follow. She worked to reflect back to Mr. B. what she had heard him saying—themes of time, policy, exhaustion, and hope—while also gently nudging him toward specificity. To make space for his expansion of ideas, she provided direct story-centered prompts such as "Looking back, can you think of an activity or an event or tool that . . . ?" "How do you know if . . . ?" and "Can you name places, specifically, where . . .?" Questions like these may feel vulnerable for a speaker, especially when the person is considering various social roles or configurations of power. For this reason, the direction and depth of the conversation should aim for the pace and comfort of the speaker. Remember, empathy conversations are meant to build relationships.

KERRY AND CARMEN'S EMPATHY CONVERSATION In the next section, we share a part of Kerry's empathy conversation with Carmen, a middle-class,

BIPOC mother of two. Carmen had recently sent one of her two children back to campus in person after having them attend a fully virtual school for the previous year and a half. We then demonstrate how Kerry used the notes template after the conversation to consider themes and next steps with Carmen.

KERRY: What originally brought you to the equity committee? What topics are important to you and your family?

CARMEN: Well, Sasha invited me. She said, and I can't remember the exact words, but she was like, "We need more people of Color on this committee," and I said okay and joined. From what I've seen, it's predominantly White on other committees. One of the things that I look for is, How can I represent my family of Color? And hopefully represent other views that people might have? . . . For example, I have experiences from my background of not being middle class—more lower middle class—and having experienced financial issues and troubles, trying to navigate schools and institutions without the luxuries of time and money and flexibility. Those are some things that are important for me to share.

KERRY: Yes. So . . . let's say you had the time and desire to organize the group for action. How would time be spent?

CARMEN: Well, I know that when people talk about strategy and thinking, like, three to five years out and implementing big meaningful change, they think it's later down the road [that matters most]. But I would also want to find ways to make immediate changes. One of the things that is sensitive, I think, especially regarding equity is about finances and being sensitive to what families are asked to pay throughout the year for different things. Some examples: the class picture and *then* a yearbook. And you know it's, like, twenty dollars here, twenty-two dollars there. But if you're on a budget? Those things add up. I saw on a [Facebook] post they're like, "Oh, I don't even buy the class picture, because it's in the yearbook," and I'm like, "Oh well . . ." (*Shrugs.*) I didn't know that, and we've never had a yearbook, and this is our first time in an elementary school, so I didn't know! But those are the things that could make a difference to a family, you know, especially if you have more than one kid.

KERRY (NODDING): Yes, absolutely.

CARMEN: What I'm talking about is the savings that would make a difference for families. I think perspective and experience and sensitivity is so important for an equity committee to think about and to have it top of mind and to just have an awareness that these factors impact families.

Kerry filled in the reflection template (see table 6.5). It is one example of how we can capture our thinking during and after the conversations.

Step 4. Reflect into Coaching

Kerry's empathy conversations happened over Zoom, which automatically recorded and transcribed the conversation—we were able to relisten to the conversation and read the transcript to do our analysis. In light of our analysis of the conversation, we identified two areas that would guide our work with preservice teachers who intern at the school. This process was an example of how our reflection before coaching can improve our intentionality during coaching. We call this reflecting *into* coaching because it prepares us with contextual footing in anticipation of dialogue with others.

TABLE 6.5 *Applied empathy conversation reflection template*

Participants & date	Purpose of the conversation
Kerry and Carmen 3/25/2022	Consider ways to bring more voices into the community meetings. Recognize Carmen's perspectives on educational equity.
What did you *hear*? Small changes to how we schedule meetings and events can make a big impact on communication. Some recurring decisions at the school neglect families on a budget and don't clearly explain the timeline of fees and optional activities for a school year. Hosting gatherings on weekday evenings doesn't allow for full community participation. Carmen used her own experiences to make her point.	**What were your initial *impressions*?** I felt like Carmen has a lot to share and is very willing to engage with issues of equity. She is not afraid to counter Whiteness patterns, such as race-evasive speech, and she recognizes that as a parent of Color, her voice matters to the collective conversation—which has been primarily White. She appreciates how Mr. B. takes the time to carefully answer all her questions without talking down to her or giving her the feeling that she's wasting his time.
What *questions* do you have? I wonder how we might target specific campuswide agreements about financial obligations. How do campus teachers plan for resource equity? I also wonder what curricular topics and themes matter most to Carmen and her family. I should have asked what she appreciated or what she would like to see in her children's classrooms. I'll pin that question.	**What *action steps* are next?** I'd like to conduct empathy conversations with mentor teachers on this campus. I would like to find out what constraints they feel when it comes to responsive curricula, clear communication with families, and negotiating financial resources and opportunities for all students.

The first area, which we labeled *tensions in family communication*, related to Carmen's comments on how the calendar matters to families, whether around budgeting, religious observations, traditions, or planning time to visit outside classroom hours. We could talk to our teachers about how they plan for family dialogue, how they communicate information about financial obligations and opportunities, and why these actions matter. Kerry shared the conversation with the equity committee later in the month. Together, the teachers, caregivers, and administrators began cowriting action steps with family budgeting in mind.

The second area, labeled *coaching support*, was related to what we saw as a continuing need to support our preservice teachers in designing curricula to represent the social identities and lived experiences of the school's families. To ground coaching cycles in justice, stakeholders' stories are important touchpoints in coaching conversations. These touchpoints help coaching teams locate meaningful entry to instruction and pedagogical inquiry.

What do we now know about the Southwest Elementary campus? In working with our preservice teachers, we will challenge them to be story collectors, too. Using critical literacies, we may ask how the bulletin boards and local texts-in-use reflect these familial stories and beliefs? What do the teachers hear in their classrooms? At dismissal? Who are they contacting regularly and intentionally? What inquiries and tensions erupt when the teachers listen with and plan for empathy? How are the teachers incorporating what they learn into actual practice?

The last area we identified from Kerry's case study was an open question: How we would know if we had made improvements in our program in the areas of family communication and coaching? The answer, unironically, depends on the families. Consider Mr. B.'s answer as a guide. How does he know if he's doing a good job? He reaches out and opens lines of communication. And if communication feels closed off, then he acknowledges that the relationship needs repair or restoration. He asks himself, "What do we need to do differently to connect in some way?" The work of empathy conversations is face-to-face work. Seeking other people's stories and honing our sensitivity to them is the essential labor.

Roles, Responsibilities, and Power in This Story

In empathy conversations, Mr. B. and Carmen share clues, or contextual footing, that help us when we are making decisions around coaching, instruction, and inquiry. And each person's concerns are very different from the other person's. Because both Mr. B. and Carmen reflect the community's needs and hopes in different ways, they embody variations of power, familiarity, and safety within the system. Their stories provide valuable information. When Kerry brought these stories into her coaching and back to the equity committee, she had to be careful about privacy and show responsibility to the relationships by respecting boundaries and maintaining trust with sensitive information. She spent time analyzing this information to make sure to identify the themes, such as financial transparency, rather than finger-pointing people whose practices were maintaining the inequity. Trying to use Mr. B.'s and Carmen's narratives as evidence of patterns in the system, or practices and policies that need changing, Kerry developed a local responsiveness that she can take into observations, coaching cycles, and planning sessions with her teachers in future semesters. This responsiveness is a form of contextual justice.

CONCLUSION

Empathy conversations are a way for communities to move forward strategically and relationally in their efforts toward justice-focused teaching on a campus. They provide impetus for stakeholder support and widen a person's sphere of influence—as someone who influences, and is influenced by, others. Empathy is related to race consciousness, both in ourselves as individuals and in our critical consciousness when working in groups. And conversations built on true empathy serve a dual purpose of building relationships within the community to counter false empathy and misguided assumptions about families and learners—beliefs that end up serving to recenter Whiteness and oppression. These conversations also help communities identify practices ripe for interruption and those important to the community.

To begin, a group must first identify the shared commitments of the individuals and the group and then use the conversations to build on and deepen these shared understandings. Empathy conversations can also help us extend our communities to include more voices in the revision of curricula and teaching practices. Coaches can support empathy conversations throughout the four steps of the process, by supporting the group in both planning for, conducting, and analyzing the empathy conversations and in reflecting strategically and mindfully on their coaching. In our case study, we focused on how a group of teacher educators, school faculty, and caregivers used empathy conversations to build capacity for shared inquiry and how they were prepared to move toward action that could make a positive difference for the learners they serve.

Finally, when we join (and design) local movements toward justice and equity, we are agreeing to walk a significantly rocky, tangled, and deeply meaningful path. We are agreeing to the uncertainty of exact destinations while accepting the discomforts, contradictions, and tensions embedded in the journey.

—— CHAPTER 7 ——

SHARED INQUIRY

Shared inquiry, the coaching tool we introduce in this chapter, prioritizes a collaborative, ongoing commitment to seeking actionable ways to address inequities in classrooms and schools. Justice-focused coaching tools do not depend on having one expert in the room. Any group of teachers—imagine a professional learning community or a child study group—who are interested in shared inquiry could use this chapter as a starting point. Marilyn Cochran-Smith and Susan Lytle challenged the notion that teacher knowledge grows from outside professional development.[1] Rather, teachers can learn ways to be more equitable in their practices through inquiry. Shared inquiry can be explained as how teachers learn by asking questions, exploring, and building education from learner-centered rather than teacher-centered perspectives.

Shared inquiry is an effective strategy when teachers and educators want to collaborate with their communities to promote peace beyond the classroom walls, during a time when learners fear the prevalence of gun violence, racial violence, and attacks on women and LGBTQIA+ people in their communities. Maisha Winn shares the lens of restorative justice and other forms of justice in schools and teaching practices as twofold: justice and peace both within and beyond the classroom space.[2] Promoting peace beyond the classroom walls means not only inquiring into instructional decisions and other issues inside the classroom but also explicitly addressing systemic and larger-scale injustices in education. Moreover, justice-oriented issues also occur at the interpersonal level and relate to the worth of everyone in a community.[3] At times, these two perspectives of justice intersect—justice is both expansive in addressing systemic issues in schools and education and about the interactions in the classroom and space for children, youth, and their families to be heard and valued.

Shared inquiry, like other justice-focused approaches, requires a capacity to ask hard questions about the classroom practices that are inequitable in your environment. We encourage you to pause and reflect on what you've learned about yourself, your stances, and your communities.

PAUSE AND REFLECT

Consider your own stances toward justice-oriented inquiry and learning along-side others. How do you define a justice-oriented issue? How does your definition compare with those of others in your community, across spheres of influence?

Continue to reflect on these questions as you read more about the tool of shared inquiry. If you are in a coaching role, we will also provide you the opportunity to build some practical tools for coaching a community engaged in shared inquiry.

BACKGROUND: WHAT IS SHARED INQUIRY?

Shared inquiry is the practice of asking members of the community to engage together and focus on a critical social issue in the classroom or in education more broadly. In this section, we will also directly address how a coach may act to facilitate collaborative capacity with a group for shared inquiry.

Iterative, Continual, and Active Questioning

Just like the justice-focused coaching cycle, shared inquiry draws on the metaphor of a cycle because it is iterative. Shared inquiry depends on a commitment to continual inquiry for and with individuals (e.g., children and families) in the school community. To move from theory to action, we used an adapted version of Myles Horton's activism cycle as a backdrop (figure 7.1).[4] Horton's cycle provided groups of people with the tools to identify inequity and to explore the experiential knowledge of everyone in the room (step 1). He believed that

FIGURE 7.1 *Shared inquiry cycle adapted from Myles Horton's activism cycle*

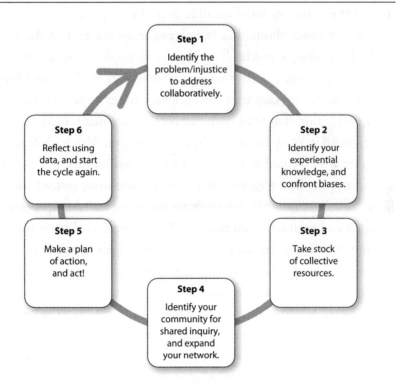

Source: Barbara J. Thayer-Bacon, "An Exploration of Myles Horton's Democratic Praxis: Highlander Folk School," *Educational Foundations* 18, no. 2 (2004): 5–23.

in any group, the knowledge and experience in the room were the key to exploring the problem (step 2). He also recognized and valued the group's willingness and ability to draw on its shared resources: books, policy documents, and, we would add, electronic resources and social media (step 3). At a point in a shared inquiry process, a group will often have to examine its spheres of influence and ask, "Who else do we need to bring into this inquiry?" (step 4). Action is key—and required—in shared inquiry (step 5): acting within the communities where we have the most control and influence. This action is important and has long been the focus of participatory approaches to research, of which shared inquiry belongs. Finally, groups engage in reflection and planning for the next cycle of action (step 6). We discuss these steps in more detail later in the chapter.

As you think about that last arrow, from the end of the cycle to the beginning, consider how each cycle might expand into new spheres of influence. This is where action comes in. An initial foray into shared inquiry may start with teachers, for example, but teachers will quickly find that their own perspectives are incomplete when it comes to addressing inequities in the classroom. Although teachers are often transformed as they engage in shared inquiry, the inquiry should not be distanced research *about* children but instead should focus on collaborative action to create more just learning spaces *with* children and families. Such action will often need to disrupt the status quo to embrace choice, voice, and creativity for learners and families in the school environment. If the inquiry doesn't directly address inequities in the classroom and make things better for learners, it is incomplete. Action also extends beyond these local spaces to broader audiences. For example, teachers often tweet about their inquiries or, in their graduate courses, share projects that reflect shared inquiries. Our local teacher inquiry group holds an "unconference" twice a year. Here, teachers share and build knowledge together. We are inspired by the idea that action, as part of shared inquiry, often extends beyond an individual community.

Focusing on Equity, Justice, and Classroom Practices

You may be familiar with the idea of inquiry as a method of teaching in the classroom. Inquiry is often used to flatten classroom hierarchies so that learners and adults can collaborate in the discovery of new knowledge. For example, drawing on their critical literacies, learners and their teachers might inquire about how the weather they observe relates to what scientists know about climate change. Inquiry in the classroom can also refer to the work of a teacher, learners, and families and communities to focus on justice. We have seen how teachers, for example, have invited parents to speak as experts when the class is exploring the history of the community and how racist systems have affected BIPOC locally. Inquiry with a justice focus zooms in on educational systems that are inherently inequitable for children and families.[5]

Inquiry is not easy to learn, and we hear again and again from researchers the importance of understanding inquiry before embarking on it. In fact, scholars like Allison Skerrett have introduced preservice teachers to the classroom practices of inquiry by engaging them directly in inquiry in the teacher education classroom.[6] The exposure helps teacher candidates orient their instruction toward social justice. Another colleague, sj Miller, used equity audits in teacher education to guide teacher candidates on conducting shared inquiry as a cohort in a secondary English education program.[7] Our colleagues in literacy teacher education have brought inquiry into preservice teacher education by asking these teachers to inquire with learners into issues of power and equity.[8] On the other end of the continuum of shared inquiry are projects that are more local, such as instructional changes or the examination of inequities in teaching practices or curricular implementation. Regardless of the form of inquiry, all teachers in the coaching relationship must focus on similar issues with the intention of addressing inequities both systemically and through the day-to-day decisions in the classroom. Moreover, the teachers must be supported while they are learning and using the tools.

Shared inquiry, as a coaching tool, follows the lead of inquiry scholars. Just as learners and teachers take up questions that are hard and important, teachers using shared inquiry ask about issues of power, access, conflicts in education, or whatever else is at stake. These issues are often deeply rooted in systemic challenges, but they are also tied up with day-to-day teaching in classrooms.

PAUSE AND REFLECT

How are you preparing your relationships to build trust and opportunities for continuous and constant coaching with others? Do you already have shared justice-oriented interests you might draw on?

Untangling the issues of power and equity related to classroom life is one role of the coach in shared inquiry. Coaches will often uncover an area of the school day of concern to teachers, families, or learners in the community. They and colleagues, learners, or other members of the community may have identified the issue as a theme when they were actively observing together (chapter 3) or through empathy conversations (chapter 6). For example, maybe a school has adopted restorative justice practices and teachers are learning to conduct circles, or perhaps there is a time of the day when a family is concerned that their child is not seen or heard in the curriculum. The coach may assist the community in shared inquiry as they identify today's issues of equity and justice and the historical underpinnings of those issues. Then, the coach can guide teachers in thinking about the different perspectives a group might hold about the inquiry. Often, this facilitation and guidance is structured as an inquiry, wherein the participants offer one another resources, ask questions together, and enjoy side-by-side learning. Further, as part of their coaching, a coach may have the tools to support teachers in looking inward at personal experiences and biases. Aguilar shares stories of clients she worked with who needed support in making these important connections.[9] The personal and the collaborative are always being balanced toward the goal of taking accountable action.

If you are in a coaching role, you can use table 7.1 as a journaling tool. It offers you the groundwork for your entry into coaching around classroom practices toward more equitable teaching practices.

TABLE 7.1 *Journaling questions for individual coaches in preparation for shared inquiry*

Step	Question
1. Identify the injustice or other problem to address collaboratively.	What is my capacity to engage with this problem of practice? How will I participate as a learner alongside other members of the inquiry group? How can I facilitate the shared inquiry so that it is focused on justice and equity?
2. Identify your experiential knowledge, and confront biases.	How might I ensure that all voices are heard as the discussion takes shape about the knowledge held by the collective? What experiential knowledge about shared inquiry do I bring to the group, and how can I share that knowledge to expand our conversations?
3. Take stock of collective resources.	What do we already know about the collective resources of this community?
4. Identify your community for shared inquiry, and expand your network.	Where are there gaps in the voices that are represented in the inquiry? How can I connect the community with additional resources? How are we being accountable to each other and this community with our information?
5. Make a plan of action, and act.	How can I support the community in making actionable plans that are feasible and meaningful? What work can I join *into*? How will we know we are making equitable change?
6. Reflect using data, and start the cycle again.	What can I model or share to help this group use the data they collected to continue the inquiry and to share beyond the group?

The coach may take a more explicit role in directing attention to issues in education and in teaching practices so that the group can move beyond the status quo and create learning communities and spaces that are more equitable. For example, you might model your own inquiry and invite others to join the work or guide others to identify their own justice-centered inquiry. Or you might offer support by helping the group identify a topic, focus, or question, but you also model being a continual learner, engaging in shared inquiry over time, continually confirming and revising the impact for children and families. In this regard, the role of the coach is to be a thought partner, a collaborator, and a facilitator. In shared inquiry there is a continual cycle of taking stock of your own experiential knowledge in the partnership, learning along with others, and pushing for change—for justice—in the classroom and beyond the classroom walls.

Facilitating Shared Inquiry in a Community Focused on Justice

Shared inquiry emphasizes collaboration, communal knowledge, and responsibility. As Joyce E. King and Ellen E. Swartz propose, communal responsibility is an approach to teaching, learning, and being that maintains that everyone in a group is worthy and carries valuable knowledge.[10] Their concepts of communal responsibility also imply that working in a group offers a collective process to promote both individual and group improvement in relation to justice orientations and educational practices. This nonhierarchical approach to shared inquiry can be challenging to achieve in practice but contributes greatly to this tool's impact.

The practice of collaborating for justice-oriented inquiry can feel unsettling or uncertain in the moment. However, as Vicky Willegems and colleagues found in their systematic literature review, when teachers, especially preservice teachers, engage in collaborative inquiry, everyone's knowledge, instructional techniques, and overall professional development are expanded.[11] To accomplish this expansion through shared learning and inquiry, we must revise how we see coaches, experts, and novice teachers, instead valuing the contributions of all members of the inquiry team.[12] Each member of the team holds knowledge, can ask critical questions, and ultimately takes action to make schools and classrooms more just places for children.

At this point, you might want to gather with your community and use these journaling questions in table 7.2 as groundwork for entering shared inquiry together.

TABLE 7.2 *Journaling questions for groups launching a shared inquiry*

Step	Question
1. Identify the injustice or other problem to address collaboratively.	What do we know about our community? What are the strengths and assets of the learners in our community? Where do we see indications of injustice, an imbalance of power, or other problems in our teaching practice?
2. Identify your experiential knowledge, and confront biases.	What experiences have we had related to this topic, problem of practice, or equity issue? Why is this an important issue for our community to address? How might our experiences or learning knowledge help the group respond to this problem of practice or issue of equity? Where can we be experts in this experience? Conversely, how might we need to take a stance as learners and listeners? How might our shared experiential knowledge help us generate a response to our inquiry?
3. Take stock of collective resources.	What resources (including time) do we have available as individuals and as a group? Considering our resources, how might we take action in the coming days or weeks toward our shared goal?
4. Identify your community for shared inquiry, and expand your network.	Are there experts we might consult for additional information as we plan to act? What considerations can we make about the intellectual and emotional work involved in supporting this shared inquiry?

continues

TABLE 7.2   *Continued*

Step	Question
5. Make a plan of action, and act.	In what ways will actions be taken by members of our community, and how are they aligned with other actions and with our problem of practice? What work can we join? How will we know we are making equitable change?
6. Reflect using data, and start the cycle again.	Moving forward, what do we need to do to continue with this inquiry and to undertake further actions or to change directions? What technologies can we draw on to move ahead with action?

As you are reflecting on your conversations with your community, we also want to share one more practical tool with you. As we mentioned earlier, shared inquiry is iterative, and you might need a tool to keep track of the inquiries that guide your collaborative work. Table 7.3 is a tool for groups to record and keep track of their shared inquiry over time and reflect together on the shared process.

TABLE 7.3   *Log template for groups conducting shared inquiry*

Step	Notes on implementation	Reflection What happened? Here, you might reflect on what happened because of the action. Were learners provided choice? Did they have agency in their learning?
1. Identify the injustice or other problem to address collaboratively.	What is the problem of practice? How does it relate to issues of equity? Who will participate?	
2. Identify your experiential knowledge, and confront biases.	What expertise do we hold, together as a group, related to this problem of practice? What tools do we need if we are to collaborate?	

TABLE 7.3 *Continued*

Step	Notes on implementation	Reflection What happened? Here, you might reflect on what happened because of the action. Were learners provided choice? Did they have agency in their learning?
3. Take stock of collective resources.	What resources do we already hold as a group to do shared inquiry? Considering these resources, what is reasonable for us to accomplish, and what is the timeline?	
4. Identify your community for shared inquiry, and expand your network.	How can we expand our network to provide additional experiential knowledge and resources? Whose voices need to be heard if we are to move forward? How will we hear those voices?	
5. Make a plan of action, and act.	What are our action items? How will we know that our actions are making positive change? How will we share what we learn?	
6. Use collected data and continue the cycle again.	Moving forward, what do we need to do to continue with this inquiry, to undertake further actions, or to change directions?	

POWER IN INSTITUTIONAL ROLES

The practice of shared inquiry will inevitably feel comfortable and familiar for some teachers and coaches and less familiar for others. To build the habits of collaborative inquiry as a team, the group often needs encouragement, modeling, and guidance. To create the non-hierarchical partnerships needed for this coaching tool, the group must give people the space to share their expertise and knowledge. But if you, as the coach, take the lead in building this space, you need the trust of others in the group. You might also feel tensions in being seen as the leader of the inquiry. For these reasons, you have to anticipate the power dynamics that come with that facilitation. Additionally, the responsibilities in shared inquiry may often fall inequitably between group members, another significant challenge you may face with this coaching tool.

How can you engage in shared inquiry when it is not yet a practice familiar for others in the community?

- We first suggest creating space, using either some of the previous coaching tools explored or your own tools and community expectations, to recognize the expertise and knowledge held by each individual. Make their expertise as public within the group as individuals are comfortable with. Your community might want to return to some of the initial questions for coaching teams in chapter 2 and empathy conversations in chapter 6 to build shared definitions of justice.
- If you find yourself in a leadership or modeling role, ensure a safe and equitable space for your community to collaborate. We encourage you to do so by asking questions, building capacity and confidence *with* others, and generating authentic inquiries that you also hold about teaching and education for and with the community.
- You may also consider creating and sharing shared values and experiences as part of the initial work of engaging in this coaching tool.

How can you focus on equitable responsibilities and recurrent action toward justice in shared inquiry?

- Engage in process checks as a group throughout the use of the tool to see how individuals and the collective feels about their engagement, being heard, and the impact of the shared actions.
- Have transparent conversations pointing out that equitable and recursive action does not mean that everyone does the same thing at the same time. However, the key with this tool is that the actions of the group and individuals are adapted and repeated for each person to ensure an impact of positive and more just change.

While these are only a few of the power dynamics and responsibilities that will influence shared inquiry in schools and in coaching, we recommend discussing these conflicts and others before, during, and after you use this tool. As in previous chapters, these suggestions are just some of the many ways in which power and responsibilities might be addressed or anticipated in this coaching tool.

SHARED INQUIRY: A PRACTICAL GUIDE

To bring these features of shared inquiry into practice, first identify the bounds of your learning community, referring to chapter 2 and your spheres of influence. Are you in a coaching partnership or working as a coach in a school? Is your learning community a grade-level team committed to coaching one another through shared inquiry? Either way, shared inquiry requires the active engagement of all members of the community. So, if you are not yet in a coaching partnership or community, you might recruit others in light of your own or others' interest in making a transformation. Also, like other coaching tools, shared inquiry is not a onetime experience but is instead an ongoing process and cycle.

Step 1. Identify the Injustice or Other Problem of Practice

To begin the cycle of shared inquiry, teachers will need to review data collected as part of empathy conversations or actively observing together to find themes and define a focus. Bringing in previous learning from empathy conversations emphasizes the topics of most importance to the community. However, teachers must also use other data available (both formal and informal) to identify the injustice or problem of practice to ensure a justice focus. For example, you might draw on town halls, other community meetings, informal conversations with children and families, or notes from staff meetings to identify strengths of the community and ways forward toward justice. From these conversations, a coach and the teachers might reflect on their own capacity to engage with these issues of power and reflect on the ways various members of the community might participate as leaders or coaches or offer support for other members of the group.

Step 2. Identify Experiential Knowledge

In this step, we want to identify the knowledge held by *all* and understand their connections to the injustice or problems of practice. When we identify experiential knowledge, we must also scrutinize our own biases both individually and in our coaching relationships. And in this step, we must take pains to disrupt any expert–novice binaries. A coach's role in identifying experiential knowledge is to propose reflection and discussion questions for the group to consider. The coach must also ponder their own role in the shared inquiry and how to facilitate collaboration.

Finally, a coach might offer support for the use of technology tools to share and build a resource library for the shared inquiry. We encourage you to identify what your district already uses to share data, information, and important messages. When they are using familiar tools and platforms, people can focus more on the information itself. As has become popular recently, Bitmoji classrooms can be a helpful way to save links, videos, articles, and websites in a shared library. Like other collaborative platforms, these virtual classrooms also allow multiple teachers or coaching pairs or other groups to collaborate using the same tools and expert references. These sites can then be used in step 4 to consult experts and learn more about responding to the injustice or problem of practice, or in step 5 to share your steps and learnings with others.

Step 3. Take Stock of Your Collective Resources

Teachers may have had more formal experiences with an inquiry, like action research projects. Drawing on your collective experiences, resources, and tools to address the inequity or other problem both disrupts the expert–novice divide and supports an ongoing stance of inquiry. There is no arrival at answers, but rather a state of becoming and continual expansion in addressing the problems. Coaches might take an active role in helping groups identify the collective resources in a community. Perhaps there are subject matter experts within the group, but others who are great at eliciting experiences or making connections between data and practice. Coaches might help a group to refine their process of inquiry based on these collective resources. One resource important to consider is time—the resources teachers often find in short supply.

Step 4. Identify Your Community, and Expand Your Network

Although closely aligned to step 3, step 4 asks the important question "Who else in our community could we include to strengthen our shared inquiry?" In shared inquiry, people often hold bidirectional roles as coaches and learners, because of the different expertise they hold. Teams that have established these cycles as ways of being will often recruit new teammates and teachers, such as early-career teachers coming into the school, into the inquiry. To expand a network, you call others in. Your community might also sometimes feel challenged to move the inquiry forward, because of time or other scarce resources. For example, to expand your network, your group might call in administrative members or university faculty who may have time or resources to support the shared inquiry. Or your group might enlist other teachers interested in similar questions. Often overlooked is a coach's ability to facilitate this process by modeling ways of seeking out support or by coaching teachers to locate expertise in the community and bring it in. Coaches can model how to honor the intellectual and emotional work others take on when consulting and how to critically reflect on how a person's position and power are relevant to the collaboration.

Step 5. Make a Plan of Action, and Act

At the heart of shared inquiry is planning and action, and doing so with intention to be inclusive. While planning and action are the heart of the shared inquiry, you'll want to do so quickly and thoughtfully by considering the capacities of the community and your shared commitments. Considering how collective actions address the inequity or problem of practice, what opportunities do you have to observe and collect data for the inquiry? What would you need to collect to determine the impact of reorienting toward equity and justice? We encourage planning and acting in the same step, as this helps ensure alignment (and the urgency of the shared inquiry) between the plan and the action.

Action can and should take a variety of forms, depending on the goals of the inquiry, the focus of the justice-oriented questions, and the circumstances under which you are coaching. We encourage you to think on a variety of levels and to consider many situations. For example, in a local application, the action might be a change in teaching practices in the classroom to better align beliefs and actions or the hosting of more opportunities to engage with families and community members to share their knowledge and desires for the community. You might consider how you would lead a local professional development session to share your learnings with others. However, you may also think about other networks you have and who you might learn from and with if you present your shared inquiry at a local or national educational conference. Here we encourage you to draw on your spheres of influence to consider the networks and communities you are part of, and how your action might support ripples of change more broadly.

When considering action, teachers often draw on technology to increase the reach and to widen the audience for action. Especially when moving to the final step of each iterative cycle, we have worked with coaching pairs to promote their findings using Flip or other video platforms or Canva for creating infographics to share their inquiry with others. We have also seen teachers host twitter chats. This kind of technology usage is not required, but given the orientations toward justice and collaboration, these actions give teachers a way to share iterations and recruit other teachers into the shared inquiry and coaching relationships in future iterations. Regardless of the specific action, we encourage you to think about its potential impact.

Step 6. Use Collected Data, and Continue the Cycle Again

At this point, revisiting the data collected individually and together affords your group the chance to decide whether to continue the same inquiry or move to a new injustice or other problem. Regardless, the decision is based on data collected (formally and informally) and the needs of the community. The process continues iteratively over time. If you are an educator, you are considering how you know your actions have disrupted inequities or reimagined the problem. As a community, you are asking whether the shared inquiry will continue to be your focus or whether it is time to move to a new challenge. Again, you can use table 7.3 as a tool for this reflection.

It can be tempting to stop a shared inquiry, especially if things are going well in the classroom. However, in these moments, coaches can support deeper dives into the shared inquiry. They might consider how they can guide others who are reviewing, compiling, or representing the collected data; they might, for example, create spreadsheets, graphs, or slideshows to bring learner artifacts or other data back to the group. Coaches might also make their own plan for reviewing the data together. As in other steps in the process, coaches should reflect on expert–novice divides and how to generate solidarity with teachers who are making changes in the classroom. Coaches may also encourage the community to begin the cycle again with new questions.

ERICA, AVERY, AND GABRIELA'S STORY

There are three main participants in this story: one of us (Erica), who is a teacher educator at the university and who also shared an earlier story; Avery, a cooperating teacher; and Gabriela, a preservice teacher. Erica redesigned a university course focused on building classroom communities at the elementary level. In the redesign, she embedded a group shared inquiry much akin to a professional learning community. Erica and a group of preservice teachers inquired into their own biases and practices and the historical contexts of inequitable power dynamics in schools and together built a new vision for a replacement of classroom management with equity orientations. The inquiry lasted several months and was responsive to the school, the context, and the individuals collaborating. The questions guiding the inquiry were "What do we mean when we say 'classroom management'? And what would it look and sound like to engage in this idea from an equity and justice-oriented perspective?" While Erica set the larger inquiry frame, each individual educator (including Erica) revisited this idea by creating subinquiries related to their specific teaching decisions in the classroom. In this regard, there were nested levels of inquiry. For most teachers, this nested approach meant working to apply their understanding to the larger inquiry question and their day-to-day practices in schools. For example, Erica worked with preservice teachers as they lived out the values and perspectives in their community inquiry, and she helped them develop critical stances and lesson plans that centered restorative justice core tenets and approaches to relationships and community.

Avery was a mentor teacher and coach and was in her thirteenth year of teaching. She also had extensive experience as a classroom teacher, an administrator, and a formal instructional coach. She was now teaching first grade and served as a district teacher leader. Her inquiry interests related to her professional roles: she helped other teachers conduct research on supporting independence for children to identify strategies in their social and emotional learning and to help them feel secure and comfortable in their learning community. She was also leading lower elementary teachers in her school to implement restorative justice in relation to the classroom community and learning.

Gabriela was a preservice teacher working with Avery for the entire year and had a passion for early elementary education and social-emotional learning. She had come to this focus in part because of her experience in early elementary classes the previous semester, after observing how children were excluded from the learning environment and how social-emotional learning was separated from, rather than embedded in, academics. Gabriela was also in the larger inquiry group with Erica. By offering a critical perspective, Avery and Erica were able to coach Gabriela to facilitate her examination of the intersection of racial and structural biases with social-emotional learning in schools. Now we turn our focus to the coaching in shared inquiry, particularly the shared inquiry of Avery and Gabriela.

Step 1. Identify the Injustice or Other Problem of Practice

The shared inquiry for Gabriela and Avery emerged somewhat from their outside interests and focused on social-emotional learning and equity orientations to teaching. It also evolved while they were teaching the same group of learners and through their formal and informal discussions. During this evolution, Avery described their coaching relationship as continuous and constant. When she reflected on their shared inquiry, she said she never waited to schedule time to discuss issues but rather saw the shared inquiry as an ongoing conversation grounded in what was best for children.

At first, the shared inquiry began with Gabriela asking Avery questions about why she used restorative circles or peer-to-peer participation structures in the classroom. In these emergent conversations, Gabriela positioned Avery, her coach, as the expert. As the coach, Avery explained her teaching decisions, always connecting decisions to the impact on children. She also often explained how she was responding to systems in which children are often denied a chance to engage fully and emotionally with their community and the content. By narrating her decisions and modeling her own curiosity with the topic, Avery coached Gabriela to align their interests toward justice. Over time, the conversations shifted, with Avery moving from reporting and answering Gabriela's questions to instead conversing about shared ways they could integrate justice orientations in their social-emotional teaching in child-driven ways. Thus, with Avery's guidance, Gabriela pivoted from social-emotional learning broadly to more explicitly connecting this kind of learning to justice, and how their classroom practice was moving beyond the status quo in schools.

Step 2. Take Stock of Experiential Knowledge

Both Avery and Gabriela held substantial experiential knowledge. Avery's knowledge came primarily from her longtime focus on this topic with children and other colleagues, her master's degree coursework, and continued professional development. Gabriela, as part of the larger inquiry group with Erica and her peers, had been exploring and enacting restorative justice to rectify harm caused by schools and curricular decisions to children and families. She had also been studying the historical context of classroom management and social-emotional learning in schools. The group's shared inquiry led the teachers to create a web-based platform containing videos and infographics for others to learn and try on similar teaching practices in their own classrooms. As the coach, Erica found ways to share the learnings on a larger platform with teachers, and she modeled how teachers could be thought partners with other teachers to revise their curriculum to reflect restorative justice with culturally sustaining and community-centered literacies.

Gabriela had this platform to contribute to the inquiry, and Avery brought her experiences from her professional development sessions and her knowledge acquired from her years of teaching. As a coach, Avery also asked questions and offered room for Gabriela to surface her observations, her professional development, and her experience as a child in school. In addition, Avery was consistently committed to being and becoming an anti-bias teacher and shared her concerns of ensuring that spaces were culturally responsive and restorative. She often thought about it through the lens of children in the class and her own biracial daughters. Avery considered and reflected on her Whiteness and power, and how to disrupt power as they engaged in shared inquiry. Gabriela identified as Latina, and disrupting power mattered to her because of her own schooling experience and earlier field experiences, which were less attuned to children's emotional learning.

Steps 3 and 4. Gather Resources, and Identify Communities

For Avery and Gabriela, these steps happened together. They found their own resources and looked to the community for support. As the two women inquired together, they developed teaching practices and shared lessons as well as individual projects. In finding resources, they identified texts, tools, and people to support their learning. They engaged in formal and informal conversations with children and families about their perspectives, concerns, and beliefs related to the inquiry focus. These conversations served as important catalysts in their information gathering and in working with the community together. Avery also collaborated with other teacher leaders beyond her work with Gabriela, and Gabriela readily brought her learning back to her cohort and Erica for continued feedback and coaching in her university course, as they collaboratively inquired about teaching through critical perspectives of love and restorative justice in elementary classrooms. In this way, while Avery and Gabriela were working together, Avery encouraged and modeled expanding their network to learn with each other and with others. By taking stock of their collective resources, Avery and Gabriela acknowledged the benefits of working together. Their collaboration positioned Gabriela as an equal stakeholder in the shared inquiry while they considered the communities and other coaches Gabriela worked with in her shared inquiry and teaching journey.

Step 5. Act for Justice

To act, Avery identified young children's independence in building emotional-support strategies and tools in the classroom and how the children became experts in teaching and sharing them with others. Gabriela created a video including interviews with children to amplify their words about what social-emotional learning and community meant to them, as well as strategies of what supported them in their classroom. She shared the video with other teachers, drawing from her experiential knowledge with the shared inquiry in Erica's class. In doing so, Gabriela examined data about the impact of the shared inquiry. In her practice, she created a plan to incorporate social-emotional learning into the restorative practices that Avery established in the classroom. Avery, as a coach, worked with Gabriela in their planning as an action and engaged in reflective guiding questions and modeling in her own meaning-making of the children's use of strategies. Avery also presented shared inquiry with other teachers at a national conference to collaborate and share her successes with others.

Step 6. Continue the Cycle

Avery was strongly oriented to responsibility and ensuring that her teaching decisions influence children through their independence and agency. She was well practiced at collecting formal and informal data. As part of the planning process, Avery and Gabriela brainstormed what they would look for and might collect (e.g., work samples, discussions) to support their shared inquiry. As Gabriela explained,

> Wellness is a dynamic process of change and growth, and it is important to me that learners are in an environment where they are able to grow and where their social, emotional and academic needs are met. In doing this project and interviewing my kiddos about the different ways we integrate wellness and social-emotional learning in our classroom, I obtained a greater understanding that if our kiddos are in the right headspace socially and emotionally it will allow them to do things in life and in school in a more positive and productive way.
>
> As a teacher, I feel that it is my responsibility to make sure that I am finding ways to integrate wellness in my classroom by examining a kiddo for their whole lives rather than for individual parts. We must have a shared vision (my kiddos and I) to create a classroom that values social-emotional learning and wellness (mind, hearts and bodies being regulated and healthy). I was so impressed with how self-aware my kiddos are, and I was so excited to see their understanding of when, and why they need to regulate their bodies.

The data Gabriela and Avery utilized is based on children's learning and participation in the classroom community. They also conducted student interviews to hear what the children thought was most important in their classroom community and practices and what the learners were hoping to adjust. The children thus were also involved in the shared inquiry as experts and members of the collaborative process. As a coach, Avery also collected her own reflections and data but ultimately provided space for Gabriela to make meaning with her collaboratively.

The tools that Gabriela built with Erica and the larger group supported the in-service teacher's individual inquiries in her classroom. Avery's support of Gabriela as a coach illuminated the importance of coaching in shared inquiry. As coaches, Erica and Avery drew on similar tools, such as supporting the teachers in knowing themselves, their biases, and their stances; identifying justice-oriented issues; focusing on action *with* children instead of thinking of children as subjects; and engaging in continuous inquiry.

This story also highlights the importance of coaches' willingness to be fully present in each step of the inquiry. The work of the coach is to do, to collaborate, and to enable others to do the work of shared inquiry themselves. Avery regularly inspected her own biases and areas of continued wondering and growth as a teacher. Her vulnerability and introspection provided a foundation to guide Gabriela in self-reflection and in recognizing that learning through shared inquiry was an important part of the process. Both coaches were on a journey with Gabriela and positioned themselves as learners. By building on their own capacities as justice-oriented teachers, by supporting and guiding the teachers they worked with, and by modeling good coaching, Avery and Erica encouraged themselves and Gabriela to pursue inquiry, to take risks, and to embrace a mindset of continual growth and improvement.

Finally, we want to reflect on Gabriela's statement about what wellness means and how she internalized that definition in her practice. She mentions the importance of having a shared vision with the children in the classroom and in applying social-emotional learning that is child-centered and oriented toward love and justice in the classroom. This sense of togetherness was aligned with the shared inquiry that Gabriela and Avery conducted in their practice as well. As adults learn together through shared inquiry, their action promotes shared inquiry for the children in the classroom. We see connections between this shared inquiry and Avery's professional development sessions on the impact of teachers' practices with children and families. We also see the connection in the video that Gabriela made with words from the children about the direct impact of feeling cared for, loved, successful, and independent in their classroom community and beyond.

Roles, Responsibilities, and Power in This Story

Gabriela and Avery faced challenges in their roles at the start of the shared inquiry. Gabriela saw Avery as the expert and continued to position her as such throughout the inquiry. At the same time, however, Avery intentionally engaged in coaching moves that made the inquiry more horizontal, and she created space for Gabriela to follow her own inquiries. These moves included involving the children (through discussions, interviews, and observations), posing her own questions to Gabriela, and following a parallel inquiry of her own. As the coach, Avery also helped give Gabriela a platform to share her findings. For example, at a larger staff meeting, Gabriela presented to the grade level team a video of her findings. Notably, Erica and Avery were able to collaborate as coaches, through different roles, to provide Gabriela the tools and feedback so that she was equipped to independently continue her justice-oriented inquiries.

The second power dynamic we mentioned earlier in the chapter was about equitable responsibilities and ensuring the actions continued over time. Avery, Gabriela, and Erica all engaged in action that allowed them to share their findings and explorations with a broader community (school, district, and research conferences). This parallel and partner work ensured collaborative guidance and accountability for all three of them to follow through on taking action and maintaining a focus on justice. The recursive nature of the shared inquiry, however, proved to be more challenging for this coaching team because the inquiry culminated at the close of the school year and they would be working at different schools the next year. Despite this roadblock, the stances they had built together and their focus on justice-oriented inquiry did continue independently in subsequent years. We encourage you and your teams to continue to find ways to make the transition beyond a single school year cycle for the important impacts of your shared justice-oriented inquiry in your communities and beyond.

CONCLUSION

Shared inquiry requires nuance and attention to your own justice-focused teaching and learning with others. It is work you will do within community to expand the community to include more voices in the revision of curricula and teaching practices. Coaches have a significant role in this process, but they do not need to have a formal institutional coaching role to be a facilitator of the group. In fact, rotating coaching roles is a further way to embed shared inquiry in practice and disrupt expert–novice divides. Shared inquiry builds the reflective practices of identifying community experiential knowledge and the questions of other community members and stakeholders, focusing on the problems of practice that are most key to shifting inequities in the classroom. And finally, shared inquiry is a process of continuously encouraging teachers in a community to look for evidence that this process is helping children and families. This attention to whether and how our teaching is making a positive difference is the heart of justice-oriented teaching.

CHAPTER 8

MAKING SYSTEMIC CHANGE

As we pen the final chapter of this book, we have a deep concern about the teacher shortages across the United States. In our home state of Texas, fifty-three thousand teachers were hired in 2021–2022, and approximately 72 percent of them were new to profession.[1] Novice teachers, in their first five years of teaching, are most likely to work in schools that serve diverse learner populations and learners of Color, and these teachers' limited preparation may contribute to perpetuating institutionalized biases toward children of Color.[2] The educators who serve these communities are often unfamiliar with the situational and local sources of knowledge and do not account for the voices and experiences of the learners. Further, schools that serve learners of Color are more likely to be under-resourced in terms of materials and curriculum, from years of the impact of systemic racism. Newly certified and employed teachers, substitute teachers, and practicing teachers who mentor these learners will all need new tools to support teacher learning and development. We need justice-focused coaching as a significant systemic change.

But you may be thinking what many have asked us: How do we ask more of these professional communities, which are already stretched to the limit? As a reader of this book, you may be thinking that these are your professional communities and that coaching cannot possibly be supported on these campuses.

We start our discussion of systemic change with the voice of Amos, a White field supervisor who works in our preservice teacher education program. Amos, previously a teacher in bilingual Spanish-English communities, left the classroom to pursue his doctoral studies. We met him in his first semester as a novice field supervisor who deeply missed his school community and its collective efforts toward justice. After reading a draft of our book, he asked us, "As a coach, I am walking into a school where I was somewhat randomly assigned without knowing anything about the community and what justice means in this space. How do I begin justice-focused coaching as an outsider?" Amos's concern is echoed in the literature about coaching—field supervisors are often challenged to be more involved in classroom communities.[3]

PAUSE AND REFLECT

When you began reading this book, what questions did you have about your history of professional learning through coaching and your capacity for justice-focused coaching? What barriers to justice-focused coaching do you continue to think about in your reflections?

On hearing Amos's question, we asked ourselves, "How can Amos, as a justice-focused coach, build solidarity with a school community, and what are the challenges he faces? What is the responsibility of the teacher education program, or system, in designing and supporting coaching in solidarity with the community?" In this book, we ask coaches and teachers to be courageous in taking action, but perhaps our systems have not been tasked with taking responsibility for justice in how we design and implement coaching within systems. What would systems that support the courage to take action look like? We explore these questions in the three big ideas that follow.

SYSTEMS THAT DISRUPT WHITENESS

Throughout this book, we have used the term *Whiteness* to refer to the Eurocentric, English-centric practices and beliefs that lead to the oppression, violence, and anti-Blackness that are pervasive in schools and teaching. It has been well documented in the research literature that the teaching force remains mostly female, White, and middle-class while the demographics of schools reflect an increasingly diverse society. Teachers who are White and those whose education has mostly occurred in institutions imbued in Whiteness have the hard work of disrupting these knowledge structures. Otherwise, the teachers will continue to perpetuate narrow conceptions of what teaching and learning look like. And in increasingly linguistically and culturally diverse communities across the United States, many teachers will find themselves in the position to identify and challenge Whiteness. Taking such a stand is difficult to do in an individualized system that privileges Whiteness and White ways of knowing. More importantly, teachers—White, BIPOC, and those educated in colonialized systems other than those in the United States—are often unfamiliar with how to practice cultural consciousness and how to learn together with children and families to make changes in schools. As a consequence, teachers continue to perpetuate the isolation and isolated thinking that happens so readily in schools. If teachers work in silos—removed from others who can call them in to examine Whiteness—the teachers may unknowingly perpetuate that status quo in schools.

Teachers need the gumption to teach with humility by recognizing all that is yet unknown and to lean in purposefully and joyfully to the possibilities of radical transformation. In this book, we suggested that justice-focused coaching includes pedagogies that disrupt Whiteness. A great deal of literature relates to teaching with responsibility, extending from the indigenous, Afrocentric, and Black feminist perspectives we have described earlier. Traditions such as culturally responsive and sustaining teaching, racial literacies, and critical literacies (see chapter 2) are all resources for teachers. To support justice-focused coaching, coaches leverage these theories and guide others to collaborate, act, and connect theories, beliefs, and practices. By finding out what injustices exist inside and outside of educational spaces, teachers can develop approaches that disrupt the status quo in schools and can finally engage with communities to determine whether their efforts have moved the needle toward justice.

PAUSE AND REFLECT

Pause and Reflect: Gather a short stack of books, articles, or other resources that represent the ways you address or want to address equity in your teaching. What are the competencies, values, and practices represented in this material? How can you continue to prioritize these pedagogies in your teaching and coaching?

Justice-focused coaching requires a system that acknowledges that equity and racial justice cannot exist without recognition of the needs, dreams, and hopes communities have for their children's futures. Although you can rely on our tools and visuals to get started, there is no specific or prescriptive way to move through steps to be successful. Ultimately, how an educator coaches for justice will vary with the person and the circumstances. We agree with the concept of what our colleague Randy Bomer from the University of North Texas called "an improvable object," a concrete representation of a practice that we hope—and assume—will be changed, revised, and applied to a range of contexts. How you will adapt, innovate, and reform will depend on your communities.

Further, we discussed the ways that expanding communities for coaching can aid in disrupting Whiteness. Justice-focused coaching is responsible to communities for shifting how teachers engage with the learners in the classrooms in ways that recognize and appreciate the learners' many resources and offerings to the classroom community. Coaches can draw foundationally on Peter Murrell's scholarship and Gloria Ladson-Billings's book *The Dreamkeepers* to promote the idea of a community teacher.[4] Based on work in communities that serve diverse learner populations and that in many ways center on the practice of Black teachers, the notion of community teachers reframes accountability from compliance to responsibility. Community teachers recognize that they are accountable to the community where they work. They are not accountable to a state's board of education; they place communities as their focal sphere of influence. Community teachers see the community as an integral resource in learners' lives and learning. They know and connect with teachers throughout the community and broadly conceptualize the notion of teacher to include youth leaders, religious teachers and guides, and the elders of the community. They find their work to be in service of, and accountable to, the community. Coaches can offer opportunities to help teachers integrate these approaches to teaching in their classrooms, drawing on the approaches that make the most sense and that speak to the existing pedagogical and community goals in those local spheres of influence.

> **PAUSE AND REFLECT**
>
> Now challenge yourself. How does the stack of books and articles you assembled align or misalign with the values and practices that your most local communities (learners and their families, or close colleagues) hold? What would it look like to be responsible to these local communities in teaching? How do you envision developing collective responsibility together, toward shared values and practices?

SYSTEMS THAT VALUE RESPONSIBILITY

Early on, we defined justice as collaborative, sustained engagement in resistance to the oppressive systems we face. Just as teachers are responsible for the mental health and safety of learners when they are at school, the community is responsible for the teachers. Recently, one of us (Kerry) began working as a substitute teacher at Southwest Elementary. She recognized that as a parent, an educator, and a coach in this community, she is responsible for providing relief for teachers who need to take care of their emotional and physical well-being and their learners. The community of the individual school is responsible for supporting teachers in doing the important work they do in the classroom. Systems must support such reciprocal commitments between teachers and communities.

As a justice-focused coach, however, you are working against a system that prioritizes accountability to certain measures of success, such as high-stakes testing, which seldom align with what communities want and need from their educational institutions. These measures do not tell communities whether their children are thriving, only whether their academic scores signal equity. Many of us came into the profession (or were students) under the No Child Left Behind Act (NCLB), which provided a set of policies and goals for individual districts across the United States.[5] Accountability in education was not new with NCLB, but the act extended and legislated how states would account for all learners' progress in schools. Accountability asked districts to isolate and understand progress across subgroups, such as gender, ethnicity, and race, and to account for the progress and educational attainment of all learners. In the name of equity, the law asked teachers and stakeholders to ensure that no child was left behind, so to speak. For teachers, with accountability came an increased focus on standards and the pressure to make sure that learners performed well on standardized tests. Slowly, schools focused on more frequent assessments and testing to identify gaps in learning and remediation related to those gaps, and many teachers' approaches to teaching were quietly (or less quietly, depending on the situation) moved aside.

Since the beginning of the twenty-first century, many schools and school districts have been occupied by outside entities and have replaced their leaders and teachers with outsiders who had fewer or weaker ties to the communities in the name of accountability. Linda Darling-Hammond wrote in 2007 that NCLB negatively affected learners of Color by ignoring the systemic issues that schools face and instead focused on testing that impaired the profession in multiple ways.[6] NCLB has a persistent impact on our current profession. The Every Student Succeeds Act of 2015 (ESSA) followed NCLB to focus more on curriculum standards and aiming resources toward schools to support achievement, but little has changed in terms of how accountability is framed or pursued.[7] These laws have asked school districts and teachers to prioritize measurable outcomes over responsibility for the well-being of all learners in the system. Although we have barely touched this issue of accountability here, we mentioned these legislative efforts so that we could contrast their aims with our definition of responsibility, which has a collective rather than an individual focus.

Coaching for accountability cannot take us far enough in our pursuit of equity. Drawing from and extending the work of scholars such as Ladson-Billings, who asked whether teachers using terms like *equity* or *social justice* center on justice as it has been defined by communities, we argue that coaching for justice is not compatible with coaching for accountability.[8] And our research has shown that when coaches have focused on equity, their efforts are in direct contrast to other powerful influences in a school. For example, cooperating teachers who mentor preservice teachers have often told us that mentoring and coaching with justice-focused tools is like swimming upstream against standards and accountability. Therefore, policy makers and administrators must take an active stance in disrupting accountability as a focus for coaches.

PAUSE AND REFLECT

If you have a position in administration, how might you encourage coaches and teachers to focus on responsibility over accountability? As a coach, how might you shift conversations about practice to responsibility instead of accountability?

The coaching tools in your kit—actively observing practice together, huddling to confer, coaching cycles, shared inquiry, and empathy conversations—are designed to center aspects of justice over accountability, but your work must be deliberate.

SYSTEMS THAT INSTITUTIONALIZE JUSTICE-FOCUSED COACHING

Now that you have become familiar with each of the coaching tools, you may wonder how to fit them into an existing system, such as a preservice teacher education program or a school district. Often, coaching has been implemented to align with, rather than disrupt, accountability-based systems. Coaching for accountability is aimed at supporting teachers as they try to meet standards for professional growth and behavior. This focus is evident in teacher education systems and state teacher assessment systems. In both NCLB and ESSA, funding and attention were aimed at providing each learner with a highly qualified teacher who was certified to teach in the area they were teaching and whose effectiveness was evident in student achievement scores. To accomplish accountability in teaching, policy makers needed to shore up assessment practices in teacher education and teacher appraisal systems to measure accountability in these ways. Those assessment practices are designed to provide structure and expectations for what teachers should know and be able to do, and these efforts typically lead to coaching that supports development in line with those expectations.

In this book, we call for something different. We implore policy makers to prioritize building communities of coaches and teachers who work together to learn about their communities and spheres of influence, over a focus on accountability measures such as test scores. We call for coaches and teachers to focus their efforts and attention on creating ripples of change that have an impact on their local and global spheres. We ask you to trust that learning and growth will occur when learners and community members are aligned, as Kerry has found through her equity community empathy conversations at Southwest Elementary. The coaching tools we shared with you in this book can be the new norm for teacher learning and development. They respond to Amos, who had trouble imagining how he could translate taking responsibility for justice as a teacher to his new role as a field supervisor in this new community. The tools focus educators on the strengths of the children and communities, providing safety for them in schools, building thriving communities, and supporting people across educational and community spaces. They respond to Amos's call to provide him with a space to enact justice-focused coaching.

In a justice-focused system, Amos would experience alignment with others in his network of support. By preparing preservice teachers as justice-oriented and, ultimately, certified teachers, Amos could prioritize the justice-oriented goals of the bilingual teacher preparation program, the Latinx teachers who are the partners in coaching, and the children, youth, and their families served by those teachers. He would coach in solidarity with a school community to broaden the scope of those competencies. He would be supported as a teacher educator and change maker in a justice-focused system.

When silos are disrupted, new connections are possible and teachers gain more power and influence to make more justice-focused changes to their curriculum and instruction. Systems do not change because of the efforts of one teacher or a group of teachers in a school. They change because the stakeholders who recognize and scrutinize injustices work together with policy makers to change legislation, policy, and practices inside the school walls. A framework for learning together in communities is needed to make lasting change. It is that need that guides us over time to spread justice-focused coaching in communities everywhere.

CONCLUSION

In each chapter, we shared stories of coaching. Alice, Avery, Carmen, Claire, Erica, Gabriela, Heather, Jacky, Kerry, Lori, Madelyn, Mariana, and Mr. B. were all coaches, leaders, and teachers focused on observing their learners, noticing learners' needs, and working on how to meet those needs in the classroom. They were responsible to one another, the learners, and, directly and indirectly, the community. They rejected coaching for accountability and instead took note of and taught with practices that validated the lived experiences, languages, and identities of each learner.[9] You saw their moves to orient their responsibilities to justice and to reorient their inquiries to the communities they served as they balanced the responsibilities of their position. Perhaps most importantly, you saw them learn. Justice-focused coaching and coaching tools are what they are—robust and nimble—because of the teachers and teacher educators who used them, adapted them, and grew them together in the community.

Now it is your turn. As you move forward, you will find that integrating justice-focused coaching requires introspection, fostering strong relationships, taking risks, and amplifying daily actions toward equity. Get started with day-to-day coaching tools and the tools for building coaching communities toward justice-orientations that are cyclical and shared. As you shift your attention to responsibility as a coaching community, you will expand your view of what is necessary for achieving justice. You may feel overwhelmed by the injustices facing teachers right now, such as digital inequity, restrictive curriculum policies, and the impact of a pandemic on communities of Color and those who are on the front lines. Do not be afraid to exercise responsibility. We are not piling on more work for teachers. When things are most jumbled up and confusing, we have the greatest opportunity to rethink and reimagine what can be.

NOTES

CHAPTER 1

1. Following Misty Sailors and Logan Manning, *Justice-Oriented Literacy Coaching: Toward Transformative Teaching* (New York: Routledge, 2019), we do not refer to the students in classrooms as *students*, to reject the colonizing history of schooling. Sailors and Manning chose "children and youth" because their audience is literacy coaches in preK–12 settings. We also recognize that learners in a classroom may be adults as well, so we chose *learners* to refer to people institutionally positioned as the subject of the schooling system. We have long believed that learners are our teachers, so we also understand that this choice is problematic. We chose to use the word *teachers* to refer to the professionals who are employed in institutions to engage with learners. The teachers we refer to throughout this book are typically full-time, employed, state-certified professionals, and we also refer to those in internships leading to certification as *preservice teachers*.

2. Misty Sailors and James V. Hoffman, "Literacy Coaching for Change: Choices Matter; Literacy Leadership Brief," *International Literacy Association* (2018): 2–7.

3. Gloria Ladson-Billings, "Justice . . . Just Justice," Social Justice in Education Award (2015) lecture, American Educational Research Association Annual Meeting, Chicago, April 16, 2015, YouTube video, https://youtu.be/ofB_t1oTYhI.

4. Throughout this book, we capitalize the words *White* and *Black* when referring to racial identities. We draw from scholars Kwame Anthony Appiah, "The Case for Capitalizing the *B* in *Black*," *Atlantic*, June 18,

2020, https://www.theatlantic.com/ideas/archive/2020/06/time-to
-capitalize-blackand-white/613159/; and Eve L. Ewing, "I'm a Black
Scholar Who Studies Race; Here's Why I Capitalize 'White,'" *Zora*,
July 2, 2020, https://zora.medium.com/im-a-black-scholar-who
-studies-race-here-s-why-i-capitalize-white-f94883aa2dd3. Both argue
for the importance of recognizing the significance of racial identity,
capitalizing *Black* and *White*, to bring attention to the significance
of Black racial identity and the impacts of Whiteness and White supremacy on BIPOC throughout history and in the present day.

5. Melissa Mosley Wetzel, James V. Hoffman, and Beth Maloch, *Mentoring Preservice Teachers Through Practice: A Framework for Coaching
   with CARE* (New York: Routledge, 2017).

6. Nel Noddings, "The Caring Teacher," in *Handbook of Research on
   Teaching*, 4th ed., ed. V. Richardson (Washington, DC: American Ed-
   ucational Research Association, 2001), 90–99; Rosalie Rolón-Dow,
   "Critical Care: A Color (full) Analysis of Care Narratives in the
   Schooling Experiences of Puerto Rican Girls," *American Educational
   Research Journal* 42, no. 1 (2005): 77–111; Angela Valenzuela, *Sub-
   tractive Schooling: US-Mexican Youth and the Politics of Caring* (Al-
   bany: State University of New York Press, 2010).

7. Emma Garcia and Elaine Weiss, "The Teacher Shortage Is Real, Large
   and Growing, and Worse than We Thought," The Perfect Storm in
   the Teacher Labor Market Series, Economic Policy Institute, Washington, DC, March 26, 2019, https://files.epi.org/pdf/163651.pdf.

8. Garcia and Weiss, "Teacher Shortage Is Real."

9. Richard H. Milner and Tyrone C. Howard, "Black Teachers, Black
   Students, Black Communities, and Brown: Perspectives and Insights
   from Experts," *Journal of Negro Education* 73, no. 3 (2004): 285–97.

10. Elena Aguilar, *Coaching for Equity: Conversations That Change Prac-
    tice* (Hoboken, NJ: Jossey-Bass, 2020); Sailors and Manning,
    Justice-Oriented Literacy Coaching.

11. Yolanda Sealy-Ruiz, "Archaeology of Self," accessed June 16, 2022,
    https://www.yolandasealeyruiz.com/archaeology-of-self.

12. Gloria Ladson-Billings, "From the Achievement Gap to the Education Debt: Understanding Achievement in US Schools," *Educational Researcher* 35, no. 7 (2006): 3–12.

13. Kristien Zenkov, "Seeing the Pedagogies, Practices, and Programs Urban Students Want," *Theory into Practice* 48, no. 3 (2009): 168–75.

14. Mica Pollock, *Colormute: Race Talk Dilemmas in an American School* (Princeton, NJ: Princeton University Press, 2004).

15. Jonathan Daniel Rosa, "Standardization, Racialization, Languagelessness: Raciolinguistic Ideologies Across Communicative Contexts," *Journal of Linguistic Anthropology* 26, no. 2 (2016): 162–83; Jennifer Keys Adair and Kiyomi Sánchez-Suzuki Colegrove, *Segregation by Experience: Agency, Learning, and Racism in the Early Grades* (Chicago: University of Chicago Press, 2021), 5; Gilbert G. Gonzáles, "Segregation and the Education of Mexican Children, 1900–1940," in *The Elusive Quest for Equality: 150 Years of Chicano/Chicana*, ed. J. F. Moreno (Cambridge, MA: Harvard Educational Review, 1999), 53–76; K. Tsianina Lomawaima, "Domesticity in the Federal Indian Schools: The Power of Authority over Mind and Body," *American Ethnologist* 20, no. 2 (1993): 227–40.

16. Cheryl E. Matias, *Feeling White: Whiteness Emotionality, and Education* (Sense Publishers, 2016).

17. Maisha T. Winn, *Justice on Both Sides: Transforming Education Through Restorative Justice* (Cambridge, MA: Harvard Education Press, 2018).

18. Winn, *Justice on Both Sides*; Bree Picower and Rita Kohli, *Confronting Racism in Teacher Education: Counternarratives of Critical Practice* (New York: Routledge, 2017).

19. Django Paris and H. Samy Alim, *Culturally Sustaining Pedagogies: Teaching and Learning for Justice in a Changing World* (New York: Teachers College Press, 2017).

20. Stephanie Jones and Lane W. Clarke, "Disconnections: Pushing Readers Beyond Connections and Toward the Critical," *Pedagogies: An International Journal* 2, no. 2 (2007): 95–115.

21. Detra Price-Dennis and Yolanda Sealey-Ruiz, *Advancing Racial Literacies in Teacher Education: Activism for Equity in Digital Spaces* (New York: Teachers College Press, 2021).

22. Terrance L. Green, "Community-Based Equity Audits: A Practical Approach for Educational Leaders to Support Equitable Community-School Improvements," *Educational Administration Quarterly* 53, no. 1 (2017): 3–39.

23. Valenzuela, *Subtractive Schooling*.

24. Myles Horton and Paulo Freire, *We Make the Road by Walking* (Philadelphia: Temple University Press, 1990).

25. Jane Brodie Gregory and Paul E. Levy, "Humanistic/Person-Centered Approaches," in *The Wiley-Blackwell Handbook of the Psychology of Coaching and Mentoring*, ed. Jonathan Passmore, David B. Peterson, and Teresa Freire (Chichester, West Sussex, UK: Wiley Blackwell, 2013), 287.

26. Mosely Wetzel, Hoffman, and Maloch, *Coaching with CARE*.

27. Aguilar, *Coaching for Equity*.

28. David P. Pearson, Mary B. McVee, and Lynn E. Shanahan, "In the Beginning: The Historical and Conceptual Genesis of the Gradual Release of Responsibility," in *The Gradual Release of Responsibility in Literacy Research and Practice*, vol. 10 (Bingley, UK: Emerald Publishing, 2019), 1–21.

29. Vicki S. Collet, "The Gradual Increase of Responsibility Model: Coaching for Teacher Change," *Literacy Research and Instruction* 51, no. 1 (2012): 32, presents a model that focuses less on the instructional scaffolds for learning and more on the increasing interdependence of the teacher and coach as they eventually move from coaching to collaboration.

30. Wayne Au, *Critical Curriculum Studies: Education, Consciousness, and the Politics of Knowing* (New York: Routledge, 2012).

31. Jeffrey M. R. Duncan-Andrade, "Toward Teacher Development for the Urban in Urban Teaching," *Teaching Education* 15, no. 4 (2004): 339–50.

32. Paulo Freire, *Pedagogy of the Oppressed*, rev. ed. (New York: Continuum, 1996).

CHAPTER 2

1. Angela Ward, "Learning Community," 2ward Equity Consulting, accessed June 16, 2022, http://2wardequity.com/learning-community/.

2. Joyce L. Epstein, *School, Family, and Community Partnerships: Preparing Educators and Improving Schools*, 2nd ed. (Philadelphia: Westview Press, 2011); Louise Archer, Jennifer DeWitt, and Billy Wong, "Spheres of Influence: What Shapes Young People's Aspirations at Age 12/13 and What Are the Implications for Education Policy?," *Journal of Education Policy* 29, no.1 (2014) 58–85.

3. Project Zero, Harvard Graduate School of Education, accessed June 17, 2022, http://www.pz.harvard.edu/sites/default/files/CCI%20Spheres%20of%20Influence.pdf.

4. Cristina S. Murrey, "More Than Just a Walk Around the Block," Texas Education Featured Stories, February 28, 2019, https://education.utexas.edu/news/2019/02/28/more-just-walk-around-block.

5. Deborah Brandt and Katie Clinton, "Limits of the Local: Expanding Perspectives on Literacy as a Social Practice," *Journal of Literacy Research* 34, no. 3 (2002): 337–56.

6. James Gee, *Social Linguistics and Literacies: Ideology in Discourses* (New York: Taylor and Francis, 2015), 7.

7. Hilary Janks, "Domination, Access, Diversity and Design: A Synthesis for Critical Literacy Education," *Educational Review* 52, no. 2 (2000): 175–86.

8. Vivian Maria Vasquez, *Negotiating Critical Literacies with Young Children* (New York: Routledge, 2014); Jessica Z. Pandya and JuliAnna Ávila, *Moving Critical Literacies Forward: A New Look at Praxis Across Contexts* (New York: Routledge, 2014).

9. Yolanda Sealy-Ruiz, "Archaeology of Self," accessed June 16, 2022, https://www.yolandasealeyruiz.com/archaeology-of-self.

10. Detra Price-Dennis and Yolanda Sealey-Ruiz, *Advancing Racial Literacies in Teacher Education: Activism for Equity in Digital Spaces* (New York: Teachers College Press, 2021).

11. Mica Pollock, *Colormute: Race Talk Dilemmas in an American School* (Princeton, NJ: Princeton University Press, 2009).

12. Tufts University, "Interrupting Bias: Calling out vs. Calling In," Diversity and Inclusion, accessed June 17, 2022, https://diversity.tufts .edu/resources/interrupting-bias-calling-out-vs-calling-in/.

13. Elena Aguilar, *Coaching for Equity: Conversations That Change Practice* (Hoboken, NJ: Jossey-Bass, 2020).

14. Evie Blad, "Confronting and Combatting Bias in Schools: Interview with Angela Ward," *EdWeek*, Leaders to Learn From, February 20, 2019, https://www.edweek.org/leaders/2019/confronting-and -combatting-bias-in-schools.

CHAPTER 3

1. Elena Aguilar, *Coaching for Equity: Conversations That Change Practice* (Hoboken, NJ: Jossey-Bass, 2020).

2. Yolanda Sealey-Ruiz, "The Critical Literacy of Race: Toward Racial Literacy in Urban Teacher Education," in *Handbook of Urban Education*, ed. H. Richard Milner IV and Kofi Lomotey (New York: Routledge, 2021), 281–95.

3. Misty Sailors and Logan Manning, *Justice-Oriented Literacy Coaching: Toward Transformative Teaching* (New York: Routledge, 2019).

4. Django Paris and H. Samy Alim, *Culturally Sustaining Pedagogies: Teaching and Learning for Justice in a Changing World* (New York: Teachers College Press, 2017).

5. Peter C. Murrell Jr., *The Community Teacher: A New Framework for Effective Urban Teaching* (New York: Teachers College Press, 2001).

6. Mariana Souto-Manning and Jessica Martell, *Reading, Writing, and Talk: Inclusive Teaching Strategies for Diverse Learners, K–2* (New York: Teachers College Press, 2016).

7. Jennifer Keys Adair and Kiyomi Sánchez-Suzuki Colegrove, *Segregation by Experience: Agency, Learning, and Racism in the Early Grades* (Chicago: University of Chicago Press, 2021).

8. Joseph Tobin, "The Origins of the Video-Cued Multivocal Ethnographic Method," *Anthropology & Education Quarterly* 50, no. 3 (2019): 255–69.

9. Angela Valenzuela, *Subtractive Schooling: US-Mexican Youth and the Politics of Caring* (Albany: State University of New York Press, 2010), 61.

CHAPTER 4

1. Carl Anderson, *A Teacher's Guide to Writing Conferences: Grades K–8* (Portsmouth, NH: Heinemann, 2018), 4.
2. Laura Taylor, "Discursive Stance as a Pedagogical Tool: Negotiating Literate Identities in Writing Conferences," *Journal of Early Childhood Literacy* 21, no. 2 (2021): 208–29.
3. University of Delaware, "Research Brief: Coteacher Huddles," Partnership for Public Education, 2019, https://www.cei.udel.edu/ppe /publications/research-brief-coteacher-huddles.
4. Throughout the 2020–21 school year, we studied as a team the work that Claire and others were doing with coaching in virtual classrooms. We are all literacy scholars, and along with preservice teachers in our programs, we came to connect our work of coaching to the notion of conferring, a common practice in process-based literacy classrooms.
5. Elizabeth Soslau, Stephanie Kotch-Jester, Kathryn Scantlebury, and Sue Gleason, "Coteachers' Huddles: Developing Adaptive Teaching Expertise During Student Teaching," *Teaching and Teacher Education: An International Journal of Research and Studies* 73, no. 1 (2018): 99–108; Elizabeth Soslau and Monique Alexander, *The Comprehensive Guide to Working with Student Teachers: Tools and Templates to Support Reflective Professional Growth* (New York: Teachers College Press, 2021).
6. Soslau et al., "Coteachers' Huddles," 100.
7. Cynthia Ballenger, *Puzzling Moments, Teachable Moments: Practicing Teacher Research in Urban Classrooms* (New York: Teachers College Press, 2009).
8. Misgendering matters: when people share their pronouns, it is the responsibility of other learners and teachers to use those pronouns for the well-being of the learner and the community. For more information on the topic, see Sabra L. Katz-Wise, "Misgendering: What It Is

and Why It Matters," *Harvard Health Publishing*, Harvard Medical School, July 23, 2021, https://www.health.harvard.edu/blog/misgendering-what-it-is-and-why-it-matters-202107232553.

9. Elena Aguilar, *Coaching for Equity: Conversations That Change Practice* (Hoboken, NJ: Jossey-Bass, 2020), 106.

10. Soslau et al., "Coteachers' Huddles."

11. Soslau et al., 108.

12. Aguilar, *Coaching for Equity*, 146.

CHAPTER 5

1. Jim Knight, "Instructional Coaching," in *Coaching: Approaches and Perspectives*, ed. Jim Knight (Thousand Oaks, CA: Corwin Press, 2009), 29–55; Arthur L. Costa and Robert J. Garmston, *Cognitive Coaching: Developing Self-Directed Leaders and Learners*, 3rd ed. (Lanham, MD: Rowman & Littlefield, 2016).

2. Elena Aguilar, *Coaching for Equity: Conversations That Change Practice* (Hoboken, NJ: Jossey-Bass, 2020).

3. Melissa Mosley Wetzel, James V. Hoffman, and Beth Maloch, *Mentoring Preservice Teachers Through Practice: A Framework for Coaching with CARE* (New York: Routledge, 2017).

4. Jennifer Jacobs, Kristine Hogarty, and Rebecca West Burns, "Elementary Preservice Teacher Field Supervision: A Survey of Teacher Education Programs," *Action in Teacher Education* 39, no. 2 (2017): 172–86.

5. Charlotte Land, "Examples of c/Critical Coaching: An Analysis of Conversation Between Cooperating and Preservice Teachers," *Journal of Teacher Education* 69, no. 5 (2018): 493–507.

6. Gloria Ladson-Billings, "Justice . . . Just Justice," Social Justice in Education Award (2015) lecture, American Educational Research Association Annual Meeting, Chicago, April 16, 2015, YouTube video, https://youtu.be/ofB_t1oTYhI.

7. Maisha T. Winn, *Justice on Both Sides: Transforming Education Through Restorative Justice* (Cambridge, MA: Harvard Education Press, 2018).

8. Django Paris and H. Samy Alim, "What Are We Seeking to Sustain Through Culturally Sustaining Pedagogy? A Loving Critique Forward," *Harvard Educational Review* 84 (2014): 85–100.

9. Yolanda Sealy-Ruiz, "Archaeology of Self," accessed June 16, 2022, https://www.yolandasealeyruiz.com/archaeology-of-self.

10. Knight, "Instructional Coaching."

11. Christine M. Leighton, Evelyn Ford-Connors, Dana A. Robertson, Jennifer Wyatt, Christopher J. Wagner, C. Patrick Proctor, and Jeanne R. Paratore, "'Let's FaceTime Tonight': Using Digital Tools to Enhance Coaching," *Reading Teacher* 72, no. 1 (2018): 39–49.

12. Jan Brett, *Armadillo Rodeo* (New York: Puffin, 2004).

13. Gail Boushey and Joan Moser, *The Daily 5: Fostering Literacy Independence in the Elementary Grades* (New York: Stenhouse Publishers, 2006).

CHAPTER 6

1. Gerald Campano, María Paula Ghiso, and Bethany Welch, "Ethical and Professional Norms in Community-Based Research," *Harvard Educational Review* 85, no. 1 (2015): 34.

2. David Lee, *Design Thinking in the Classroom: Easy-to-Use Teaching Tools to Foster Creativity, Encourage Innovation, and Unleash Potential in Every Student* (New York: Simon and Schuster, 2018), describes a project in which children interviewed local business owners, community members, and other kids to develop a problem statement to guide their community redesign project. When the elementary-aged children noted, for example, that community members were leaving the neighborhood for many services, the children had uncovered a problem space for community developers to address. Empathy interviews are also a cornerstone of design projects at Stanford's d.school (https://dschool.stanford.edu) a program that supports university students in developing design thinking as applied to education and other fields.

3. Anthony S. Bryk, Louis M. Gomez, Alicia Grunow, and Paul G. LeMahieu, *Learning to Improve: How America's Schools Can Get Better at Getting Better* (Cambridge, MA: Harvard Education Press, 2015).

4. Charles L. Briggs, "Interview, Power/Knowledge, and Social Inequality," in *Handbook of Interview Research: Context and Method*, ed. F. Gubrium and J.A. Holstein (Thousand Oaks, CA: SAGE, 2002): 911–22.

5. Brené Brown, *Braving the Wilderness: The Quest for True Belonging and the Courage to Stand Alone* (New York: Random House, 2017).

6. Zeus Leonardo, *Race, Whiteness, and Education* (New York: Routledge, 2009).

7. Chezare A. Warren, "Conflicts and Contradictions: Conceptions of Empathy and the Work of Good-Intentioned Early Career White Female Teachers," *Urban Education* 50, no. 5 (2015): 572–600; Sherry Marx and Lisa Pray, "Living and Learning in Mexico: Developing Empathy for English Language Learners Through Study Abroad," *Race Ethnicity and Education* 14, no.4 (2011): 507–35.

8. District demographic data from Austin Independent School District, "District Demographics: Our District by the Numbers," accessed October 25, 2022, https://www.austinisd.org/planning-asset -management/district-demographics.

9. Floyd Cobb and John Krownapple, *Belonging Through a Culture of Dignity: The Keys to Successful Equity Implementation* (San Diego: Mimi & Todd Press, 2019).

10. Bavu Blakes and Ellison Blakes, *El's Mirror* (Hip Hop Grew Up, 2021), https://www.hiphopgrewup.com/.

11. Texas House Bill 4545, 87th Legislature, 2021 Reg. Sess., https:// legiscan.com/TX/bill/HB4545/2021.

12. Texas House Bill 3, 87th Legislature, 2021 Reg. Sess., https:// legiscan.com/TX/bill/HB3/2021.

CHAPTER 7

1. Susan Lytle and Marilyn Cochran-Smith, "Teacher Research as a Way of Knowing," *Harvard Educational Review* 62, no. 4 (1992): 447–75.

2. Maisha T. Winn, *Justice on Both Sides: Transforming Education Through Restorative Justice* (Cambridge, MA: Harvard Education Press, 2018).

3. Dorothy Vaandering, "Implementing Restorative Justice Practice in Schools: What Pedagogy Reveals," *Journal of Peace Education* 11, no. 1 (2014): 64–80.

4. Barbara J. Thayer-Bacon, "An Exploration of Myles Horton's Democratic Praxis: Highlander Folk School," *Educational Foundations* 18, no. 2 (2004): 5–23.

5. Deborah Loewenberg Ball and David K. Cohen, "Developing Practice, Developing Practitioners: Toward a Practice-Based Theory of Professional Education," *Teaching as the Learning Profession: Handbook of Policy and Practice* 1 (1999): 3–22.

6. Allison Skerrett, "'There's Going to Be Community. There's Going to Be Knowledge': Designs for Learning in a Standardised Age," *Teaching and Teacher Education* 26, no. 3 (2010): 648–55.

7. sj Miller, "Cultivating a Disposition for Sociospatial Justice in English Teacher Preparation," *Teacher Education and Practice* 27, no. 1 (2014): 44–74. The equity audit is a complex tool to implement. This large-scale inquiry and data-collecting tool analyzes systemic oppression and barriers that exist for children and families. Additionally, equity audits identify relevant actionable opportunities that may be implemented by teachers, community members, administrative teams, or other stakeholders. While this chapter does not go into depth about equity audits, we do have a few observations. The audits are closely related to shared inquiry and to disrupting the status quo in education, which is inherently power-laden and inequitable for children and families who do not identify as White, cis-gender, able, and middle class. Equity audits are a tremendous tool for shared inquiry and identifying areas of focus for justice-oriented change in your practice and schools. Research has emphasized the benefits of equity audits to increase educators' ability to analyze data, increase their awareness of the complexity of equity issues, and build educators' long-term stances as change agents. The two resources we most commonly turn to are Terrance L. Green, "Community-Based Equity Audits: A Practical Approach for Educational Leaders to Support Equitable Community-School Improvements," *Educational*

Administration Quarterly 53, no. 1 (2017): 3–39; and Elena Aguilar, *Coaching for Equity: Conversations That Change Practice* (Hoboken, NJ: Jossey-Bass, 2020).

8. Ball and Cohen, "Practice-Based Theory of Professional Education."

9. Aguilar, *Coaching for Equity*.

10. Joyce E. King and Ellen E. Swartz, *The Afrocentric Praxis of Teaching for Freedom: Connecting Culture to Learning* (New York: Routledge, 2015).

11. Vicky Willegems, Els Consuegra, Katrien Struyven, and Nadine Engles, "Teacher and Pre-Service Teachers as Partners in Collaborative Teacher Research: A Systematic Literature Review," *Teaching and Teacher Education* 64 (2017): 230–45.

12. Ken Zeichner, "Rethinking the Connections Between Campus Courses and Field Experiences in College- and University-Based Teacher Education," *Journal of Teacher Education* 61, no. 1–2 (2010): 89–99.

CHAPTER 8

1. Talia Richman, "1 in 5 New Texas Teachers Were Hired Without Certification Last Year, *Dallas Morning News*, September 22, 2022, https://www.dallasnews.com/news/education/2022/09/22/1-in-5 -new-texas-teachers-werent-certified-last-year/.

2. Linda Darling-Hammond, "How Teacher Education Matters," *Journal of Teacher Education* 51, no. 3 (2000): 166–73.

3. Jennifer Lin Russell, Richard Correnti, Mary Kay Stein, Ally Thomas, Victoria Bill, and Laurie Speranzo, "Mathematics Coaching for Conceptual Understanding: Promising Evidence Regarding the Tennessee Math Coaching Model," *Educational Evaluation and Policy Analysis* 42, no. 3 (2020): 439–66.

4. Peter C. Murrell Jr., *The Community Teacher: A New Framework for Effective Urban Teaching* (New York: Teachers College Press, 2001); Gloria Ladson-Billings, *The Dreamkeepers: Successful Teachers of African American Children* (San Francisco: Jossey-Bass, 2009).

5. Robert L. Linn, Eva L. Baker, and Damian W. Betebenner, "Account-ability Systems: Implications of Requirements of the No Child Left Behind Act of 2001," *Educational Researcher* 31, no. 6 (2002): 3–16.

6. Linda Darling-Hammond, "Race, Inequality and Educational Ac-countability: The Irony of 'No Child Left Behind,'" *Race Ethnicity and Education* 10, no. 3 (2007): 245–60.

7. US Senate, "Every Student Succeeds Act (ESSA 2015)," S. 1177 (114th Congr.) (2015–2017). *Pub.L.* 114–95.

8. Gloria Ladson-Billings, "Justice . . . Just Justice," Social Justice in Ed-ucation Award (2015) lecture, American Educational Research Asso-ciation Annual Meeting, Chicago, April 16, 2015, https://youtu.be /ofB_t1oTYhI.

9. In our own teaching and coaching, we have found Gholnecsar E. Muhammad, *Cultivating Genius and Joy in Education Through Histori-cally Responsive Literacy* (New York: Scholastic, 2020), and other texts written by literacy scholars of Color to guide our coaching toward the visions—both historical and contemporary—of diverse racial and ethnic groups.

ACKNOWLEDGMENTS

Many partners have encouraged our thinking about justice-focused coaching. We thank Dr. Jim Hoffman and Dr. Beth Maloch and the research team at University of Texas at Austin who thoughtfully (and lovingly) nurtured the Coaching with CARE framework within the community of a teacher education program at the university. And to the researchers, teachers, and young people named or unnamed in this book: your endeavors in the classroom, your work toward justice, and your vision for more inclusive coaching in community are the foundation of this book.

We acknowledge the countless others who have been our coaches and mentors, those in formal and informal roles, younger and older, throughout our careers. You have influenced who we are as educators and coaches. The compilation of your guidance and interactions continues to influence our work and decision-making. We give special thanks to the generosity of those who shared the stories that we included in this book. Thank you for being our research partners in this ongoing work.

We also acknowledge the partiality of this project, this book, and our ongoing work. As we put forth ideas, through Western academic traditions, we do so fully conscious of the colonizing history and interpretations of offering our writing as expertise in the field of education. These notions—the academy, expertise, colonialism—should always be suspect in any call toward justice. We acknowledge the harm that research and researchers have caused BIPOC communities, and we recognize that as participants in this research, we sometimes continue to cause harm when we enter communities to do research.

In this book, we've tried to tend to this problem. Our work does not abolish racist, oppressive systems—that is the work for all of us, from various locales. But it does reframe ways of interacting with communities, colleagues, and instructional practices. This reframing is continual and unfinished in terms of our ways of knowing, doing, and being in the world. The book you hold in your hands is an imperfect offering toward solidarity but one that we feel can add to the conversation. For instance, one of our definitions of justice-focused coaching insists on the rejection of traditional constructions of power in our roles, and as we try to do so in these chapters and step back as knowers, we make space for a different type of responsibility. We look forward to the tensions and puzzles this reframing demands.

Jayne Fargnoli, thank you for believing in this book. During very isolated times for us as writers, you continued to elicit and value the stories we had to tell. Your recommendation to align our writing with our intentions—to write a book that teachers, school leaders, and teacher educators would find practical and applicable to their work—led to good, positive struggles for us as a writing team. At each turn, your advice was spot-on. Thank you for your encouragement, guidance, and persistence. Thank you to the anonymous reviewers who thoughtfully nudged us toward more expansive and authentic notions of communities in coaching and the editorial board at Harvard Education Press for your thoughtful questions. We hope you find that the book we wrote also reflects your commitment to equity and justice.

ABOUT THE AUTHORS

MELISSA MOSLEY WETZEL is a professor of Language and Literacy Studies in the Department of Curriculum and Instruction at the University of Texas at Austin. She also currently serves as department chair. Her scholarship focuses on the preparation of teachers in literacy for equity-focused practices and the development of justice-focused coaching and mentoring in preservice and in-service settings. She draws from critical race scholarship and culturally sustaining pedagogy frameworks to prepare teachers within field-based literacy teaching experiences. She is also interested in critical literacy learning across the lifespan, particularly how teachers and learners together design literacy practices that are transformative. She draws on qualitative methods in her work, primarily critical discourse analysis and ethnography. Dr. Wetzel teaches courses in elementary literacy methods, reading development, coaching and mentoring, literacy leadership, sociolinguistics, teacher inquiry, and critical approaches to studying classroom discourse. She is a coauthor of the book *Mentoring Preservice Teachers Through Practice: A Framework for Coaching with CARE* (Routledge, 2017) as well as journal articles in *Reading Research Quarterly, Teaching and Teacher Education, and Journal of Literacy Research, among others.*

ERICA HOLYOKE is an assistant professor in responsive literacy education at the University of Colorado Denver. She teaches undergraduate and graduate courses on literacy. Her focus is on building equitable and inclusive literacy learning communities. Erica's research prioritizes culturally sustaining pedagogy; anti-racist approaches to literacy, activism, and the intersection of love and learning in early elementary schools; and preservice and in-service teacher development. Erica is interested in how teachers and young children build community and belonging through literacy, and the literate identities and agency exercised in classrooms in an educational climate that prioritizes outcomes and accountability. Her scholarship seeks to examine the communal and collaborative aspects of learning especially connected to comprehension, meaning making, and writing. Another ongoing project includes critical content analysis and the use of picture books portraying narratives of activism. Before her work as a teacher educator, Erica taught early elementary and special education classes and served as an assistant principal, a literacy coach, and a literacy coordinator. She is forever learning from the brilliance of young children and the passionate and innovative teachers she is privileged to work with. She hopes for many more opportunities to learn and grow as an educator in the years to come.

KERRY H. ALEXANDER is a doctoral candidate in Language and Literacy Studies at the University of Texas at Austin. She is an artist, writer, university instructor, and literacy researcher dedicated to community-centered inquiry and responsive pedagogical design in elementary literacy classrooms. For 10 years prior to pursuing her PhD, Ms. Alexander taught fourth grade language arts and reading. As a classroom literacy teacher, she endeavored to put learners' identity-safety at the center of her practice. Through critical, multimodal, and inquiry-based pedagogies, she embodies what she calls an act of *language artistry*: the relational, multimodal, meaning-making involved in designing for a more inclusive world. Recent projects include a self-produced podcast series, *Coaching with Kerry*, focusing on community-teacher voices and stories, design-development research on what it means to *Coach for Justice* with the Raise Your Hand Texas Foundation, two public artwork showings, and a two-year appointment as equity chair at the local elementary school. Gathering monthly with caregivers, teachers, and administrators to organize for educational equity, Ms. Alexander asks: *What is the community's vision for equity in literacy classrooms? What discourses shape conceptions of care, equity, and success in these spaces?*

HEATHER DUNHAM is an assistant professor of literacy at Clemson University. Prior to her work in a university setting, Heather was a second- and third-grade classroom teacher serving English language learners in Nashville, TN. Her work with multicultural and multilingual elementary students led to her interest in culturally sustaining pedagogies in the literacy classroom. Heather's current work is situated in noticing, naming, and expanding these culturally sustaining literacy practices with preservice teachers. To do this, Heather draws on critical, pluralistic approaches to literacy instruction that centers multiple modes, multiple cultures, and multiple languages in the developmental process of learning to read and write. Heather believes in the importance of clinical-field based learning experiences for preservice teachers and tries out new and innovative coaching practices in her role as a field supervisor. Working with and alongside preservice teachers and elementary students brings Heather so much joy and she hopes to return this joy to the communities she serves. Her work can be found in literacy journals such as *The Reading Teacher* and *Literacy Research: Theory, Method, Practice.*

CLAIRE COLLINS is a doctoral candidate in language and literacy studies at the University of Texas at Austin. Before starting at UT Austin, she taught language arts to middle and high school students in urban Catholic schools in Los Angeles and Dallas. Currently, she strives to build humanizing partnerships with preservice teachers and base the relationships on dialogue and trust. She hopes to keep learning and growing with preservice teachers in the future. She is also interested in how secondary language arts teachers decide on which texts to include in their classrooms, especially how teachers navigate and push back against efforts to ban or censor books in high school settings. Other projects include examining how preservice teachers use social media to make meaning about their teaching beliefs and how to strengthen the network of support for preservice teachers in university teacher education programs.

INDEX